Copyright 2017 Marilyn Henrion

ISBN-13:978-1546996071

ISBN-10:1546996079

marilynhenrion@mac.com   www.marilynhenrion.com

Published by thesohobookie.com

Photography : Jean Vong

Patchwork City

Linen Collages   2015-2017

MARILYN HENRION

CONTENTS

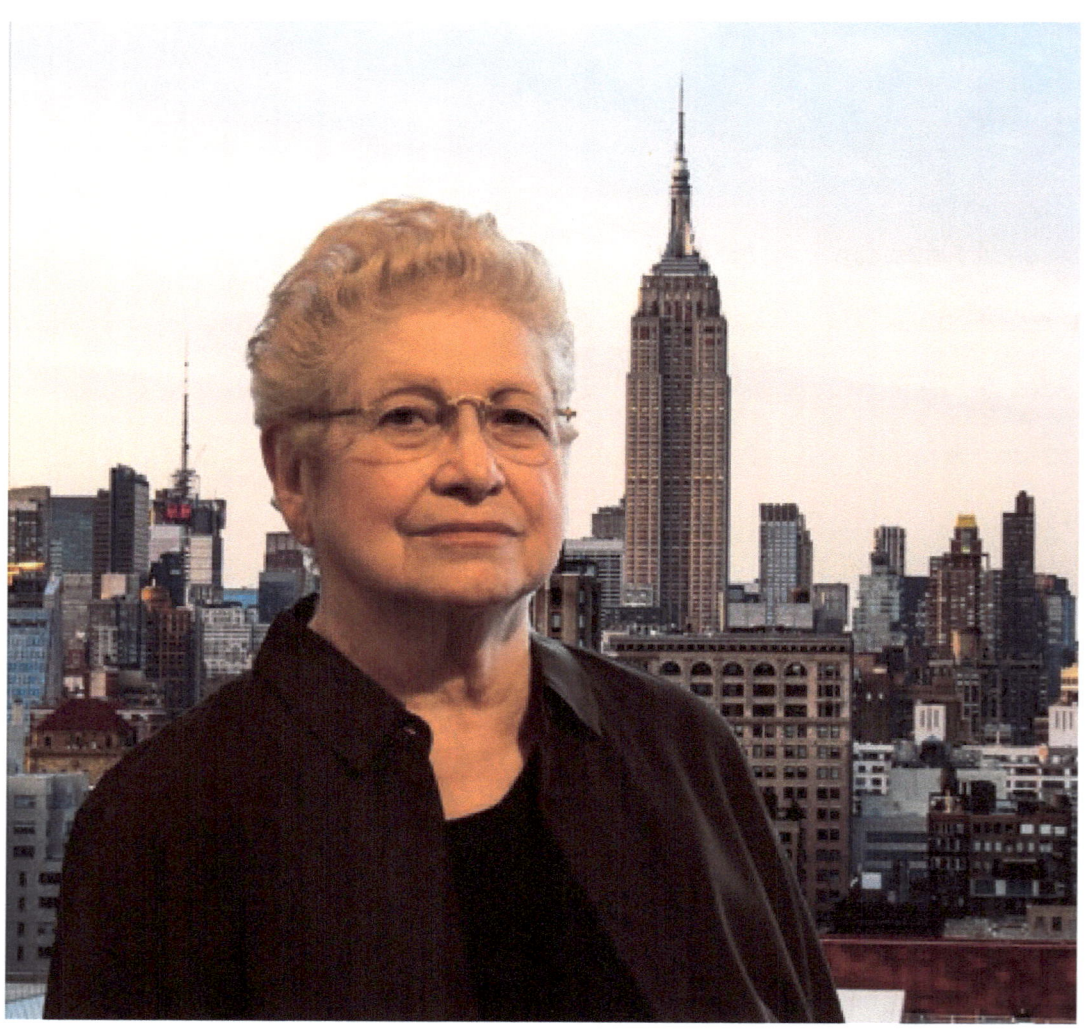

photo: Dan Earle

INTRODUCTION

As a life-long New Yorker, Marilyn Henrion's aesthetic vision has always been deeply rooted in the urban geometry of her surroundings, from her earlier hand-quilted geometric abstractions to the more recent mixed media works. The Patchwork City series, created between 2015 and 2017, captures the energy and vitality of the ever-changing urban landscape.

The new works are composed of the artist's own digitally manipulated architectural photographs which are pigment-printed on linen, cut apart and reassembled to create collages on stretched canvas. Some also incorporate hand quilting on silk, a technique present in her earlier works. Often focusing on the "window" and its metaphorical implications, Henrion transforms the "facts" of the material world to reflect her own experience of a particular place, much as Edward Hopper had done in the last century.

Of these works, art journalist Bobbie Leigh, writes, "The Patchwork City series is another example of the artist's free play with bold collage and audacious colors….Their pulsating rhythms come from a barrage of images of architectural fragments in brilliant colors reflecting how we often see skyscrapers. Each conveys the speed and compositional complexity of cities everywhere."

The images in this series are also available as custom-sized limited edition museum-quality prints on a variety of substrates, including archival paper, aluminum, canvas, and wood.

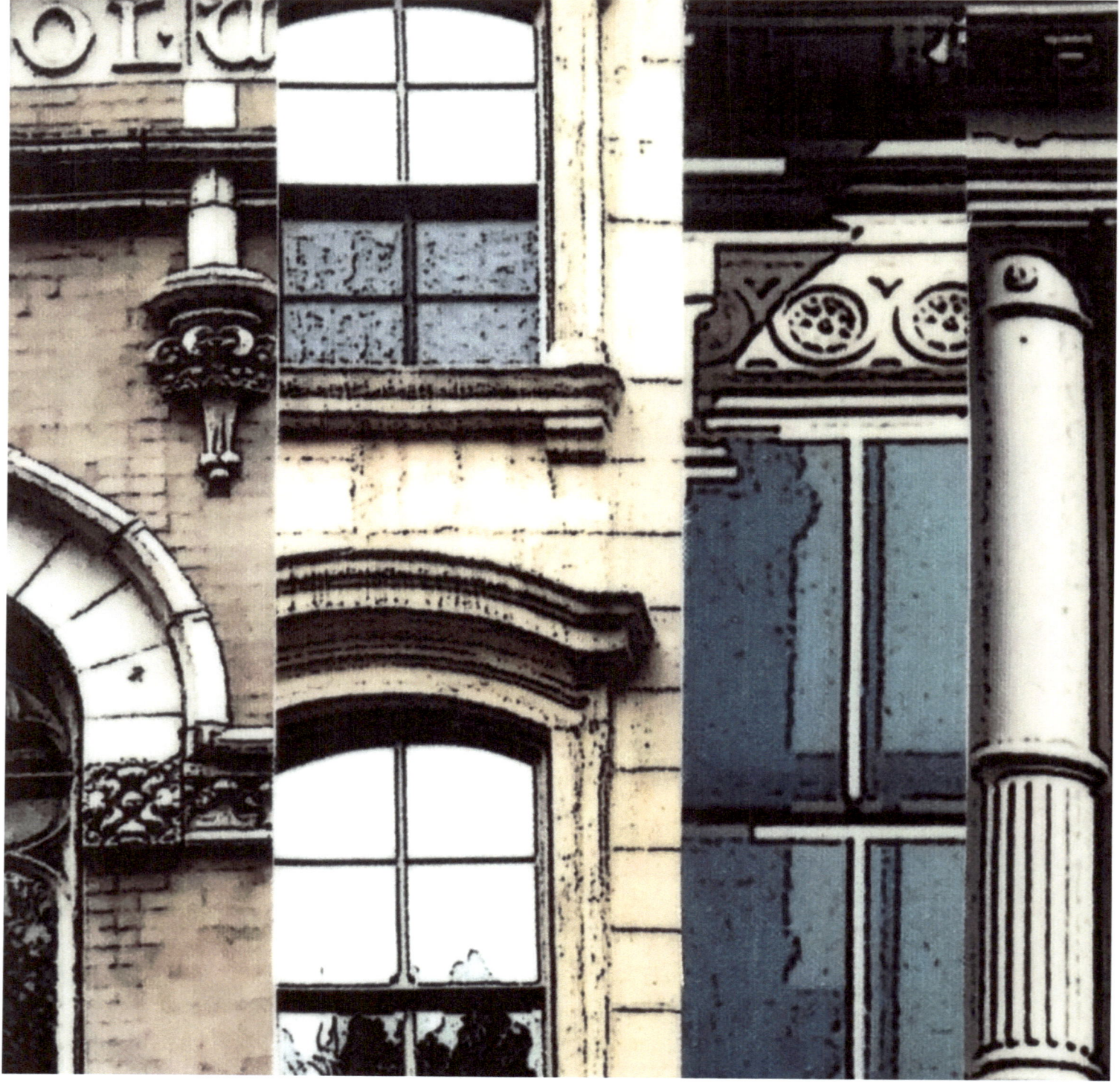

8

detail

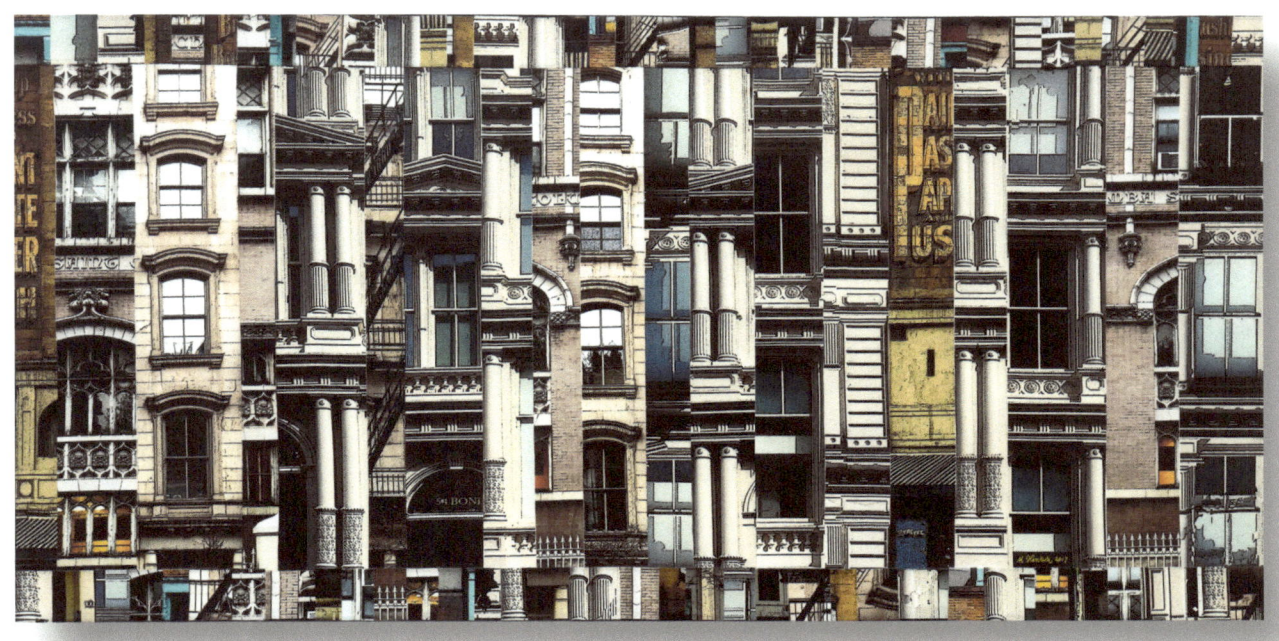

Patchwork City 73.
24"x48". digitally manipulated photography, pigment printing on linen, collage on stretched canvas

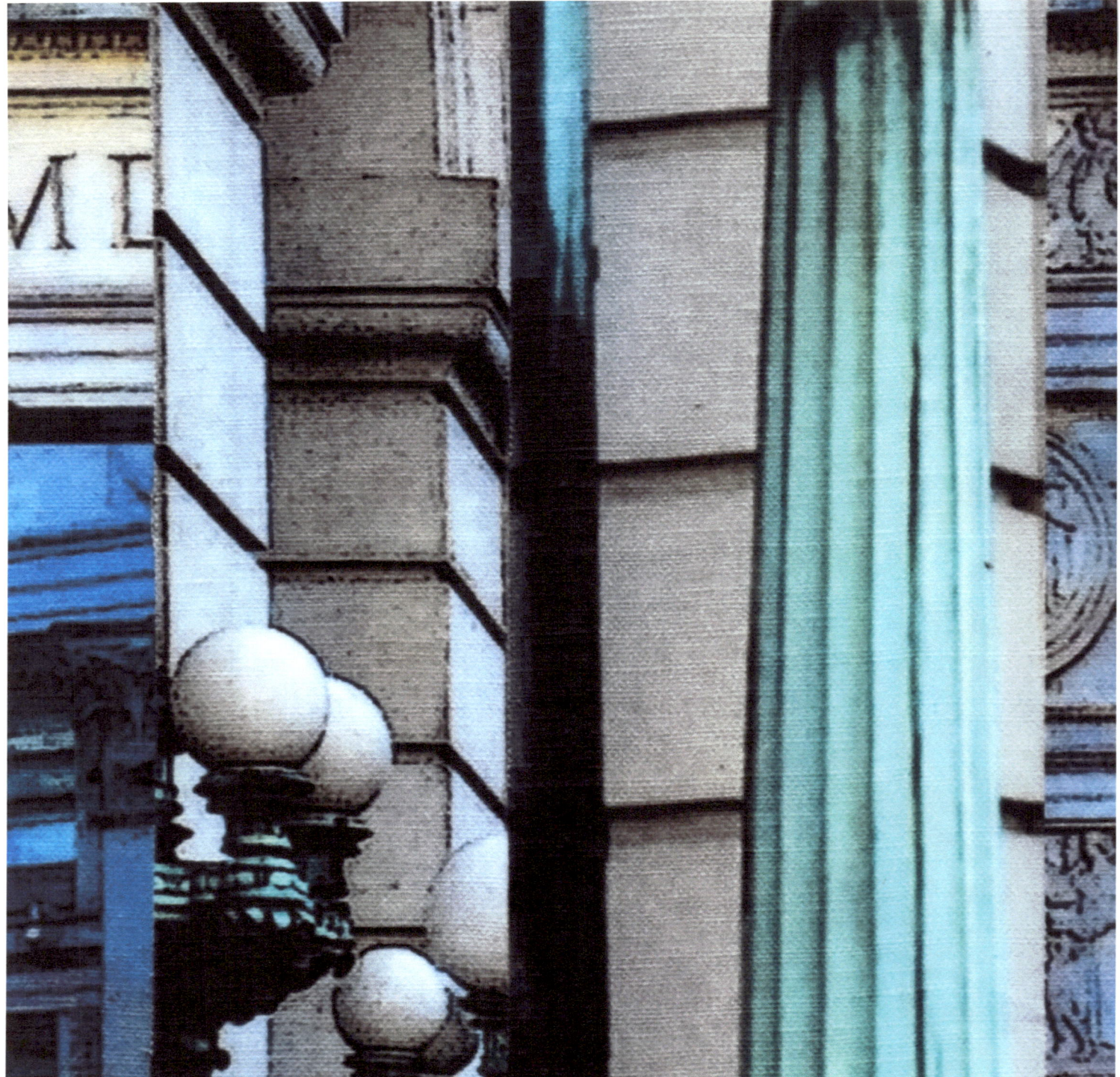

detail

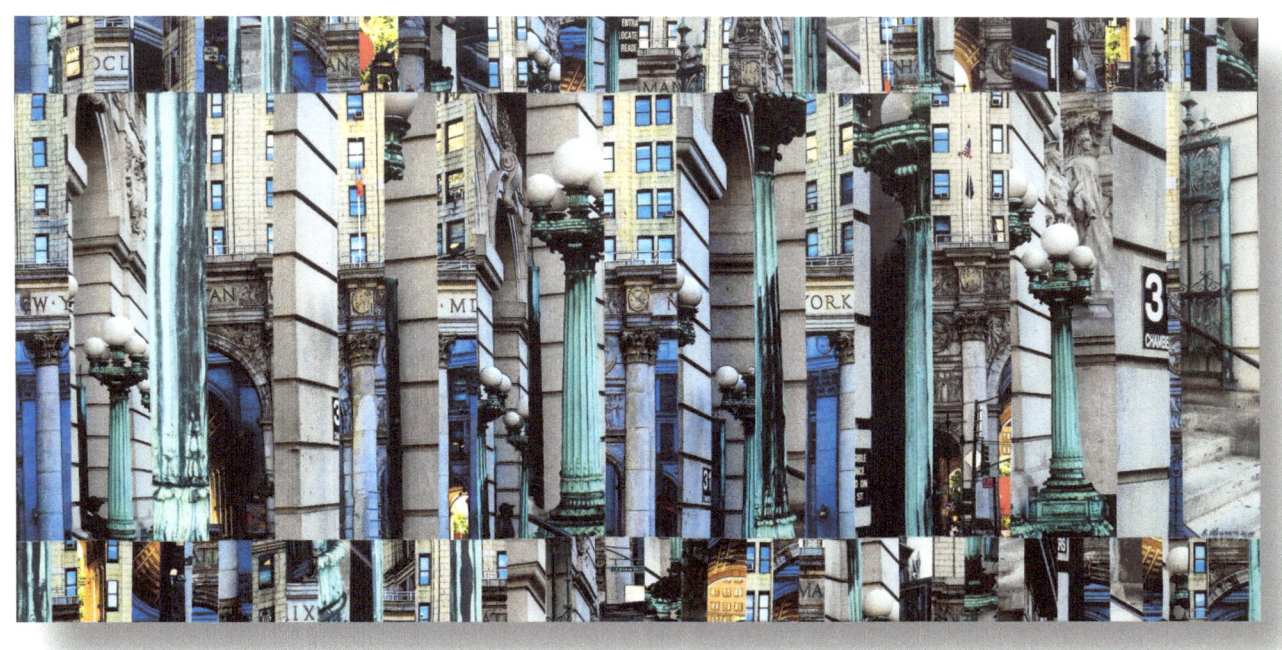

Patchwork City 62.
24"x48"   digitally manipulated photography, pigment printing on linen, collage on stretched canvas

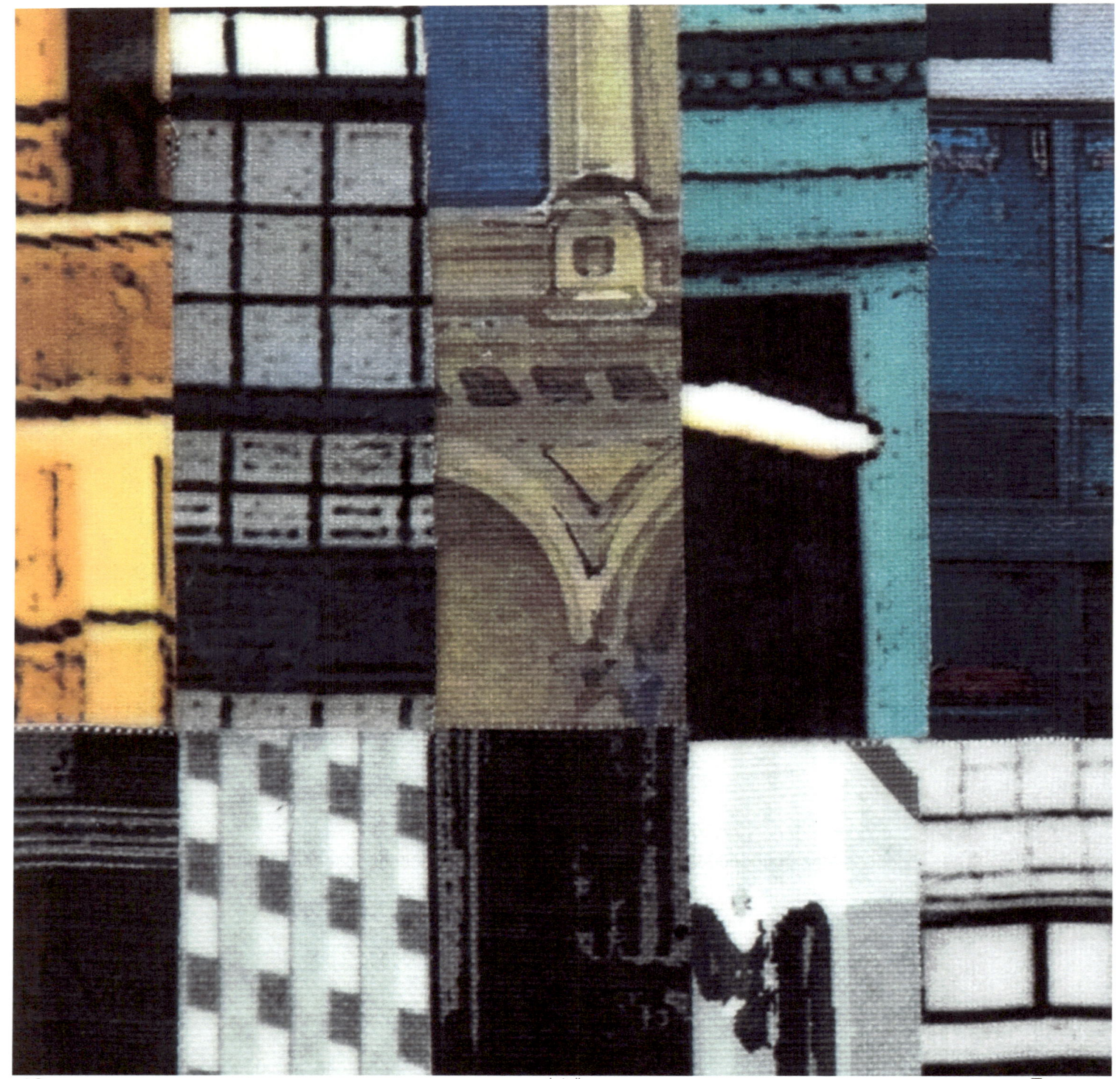

detail

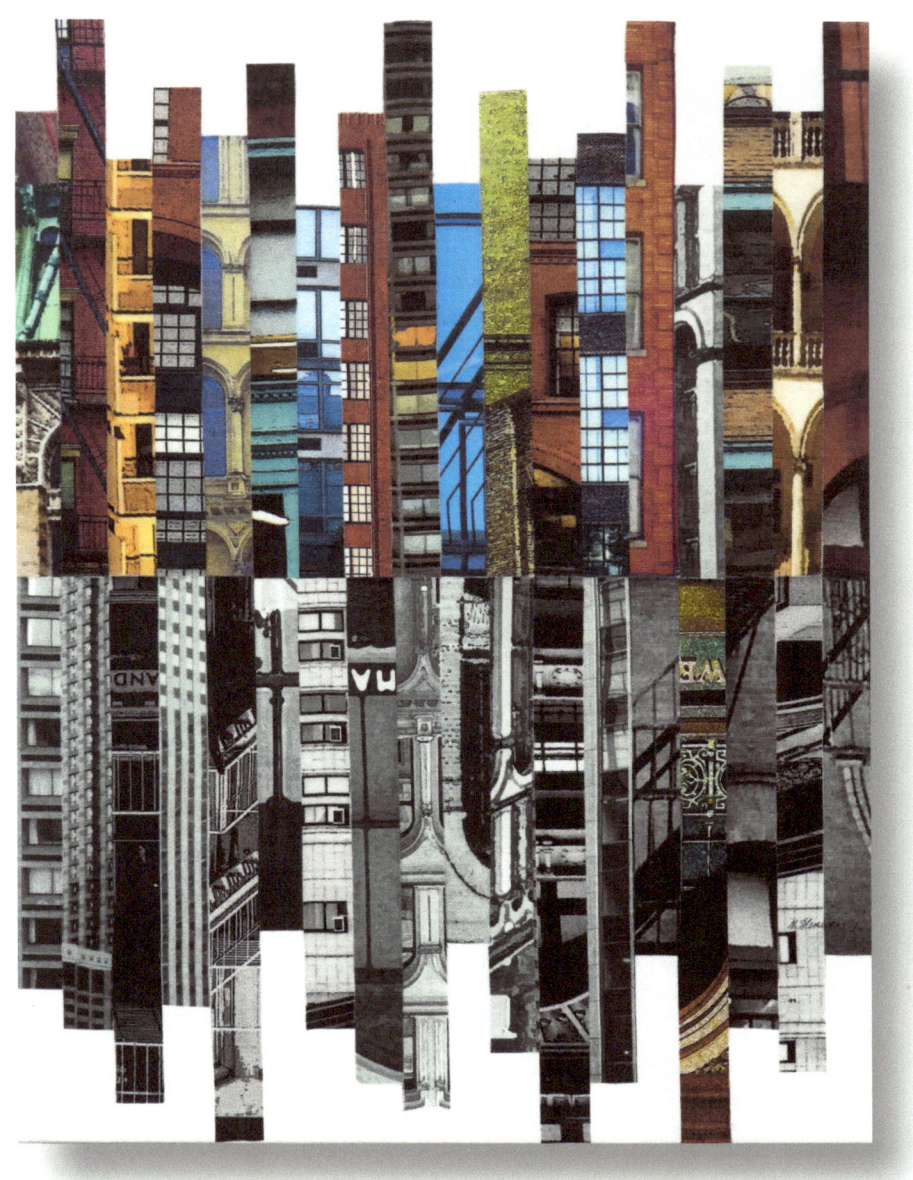

Patchwork City 72.
24"x18". digitally manipulated photography, pigment printing on linen, collage on stretched canvas

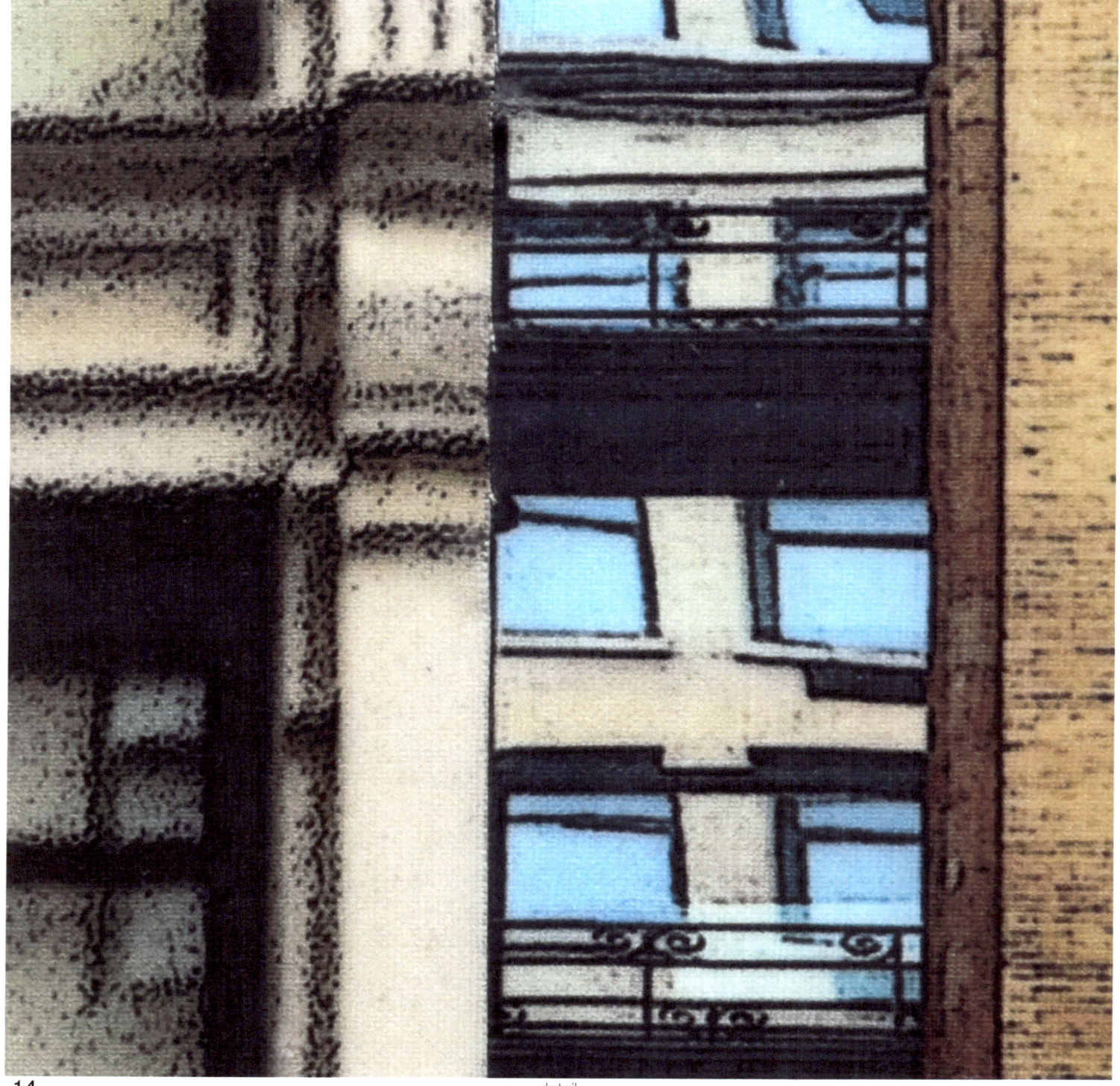

14   detail

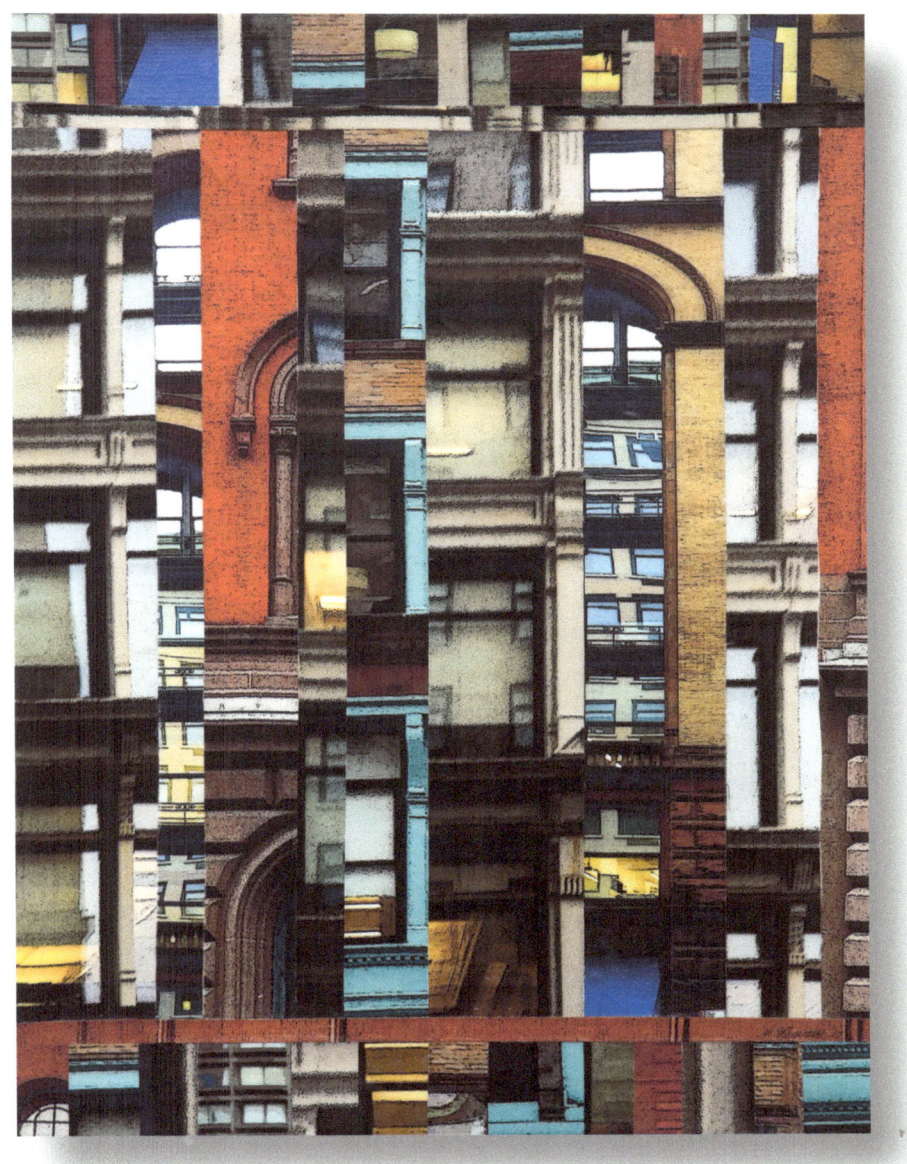

Patchwork City 71
24"x18". digitally manipulated photography, pigment printing on linen, collage on stretched canvas

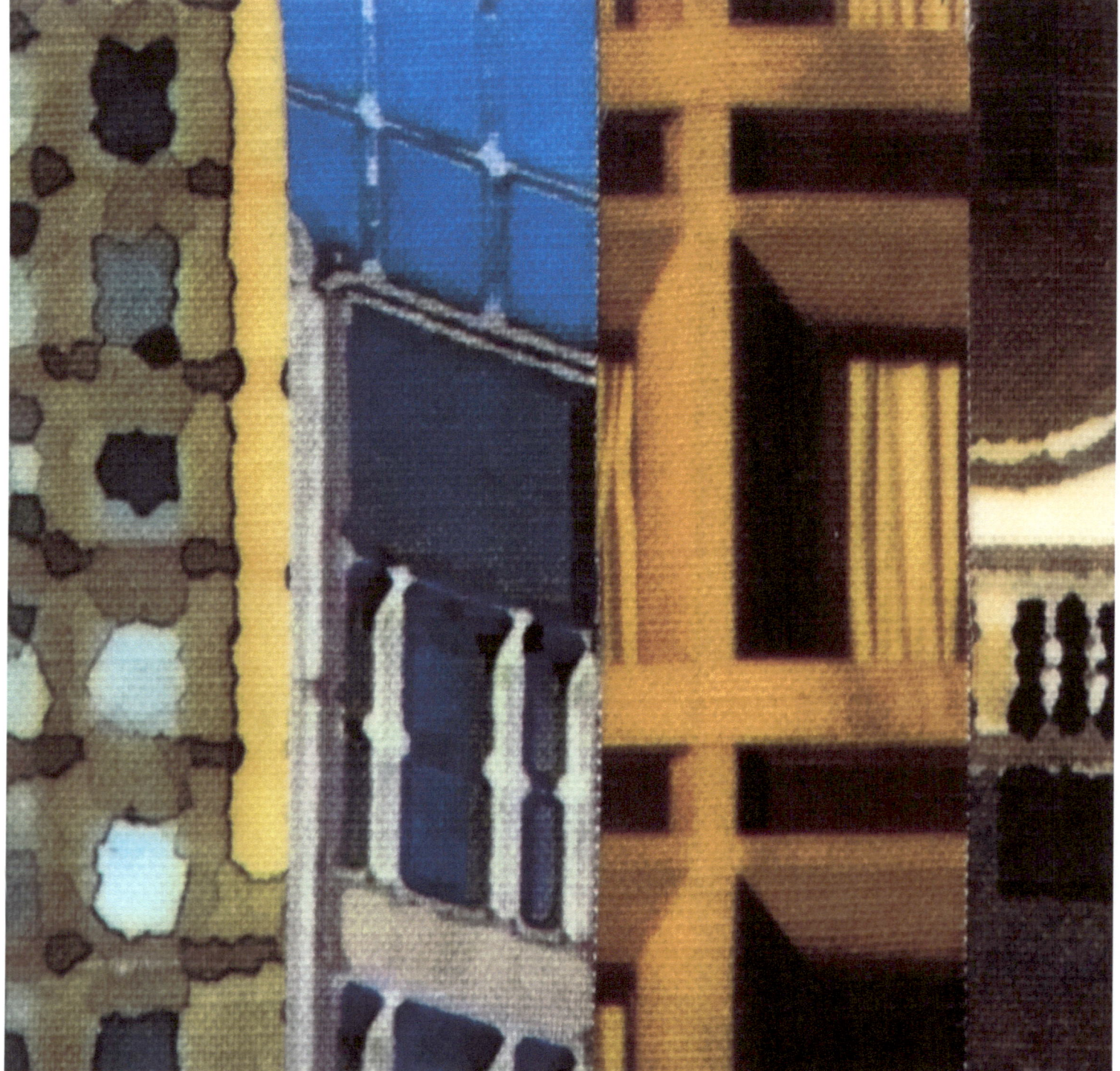

detail

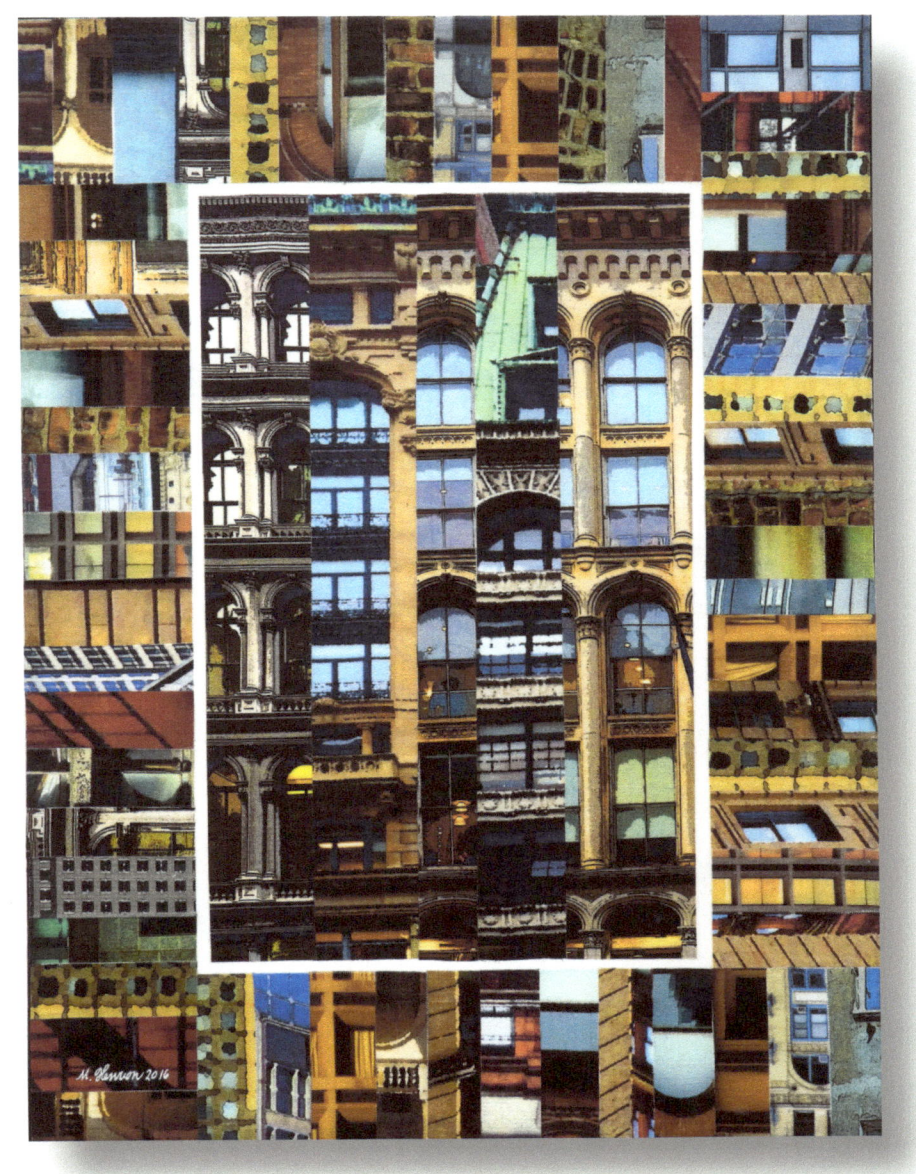

Patchwork City 69
24"x18". digitally manipulated photography, pigment printing on linen, collage on stretched canvas

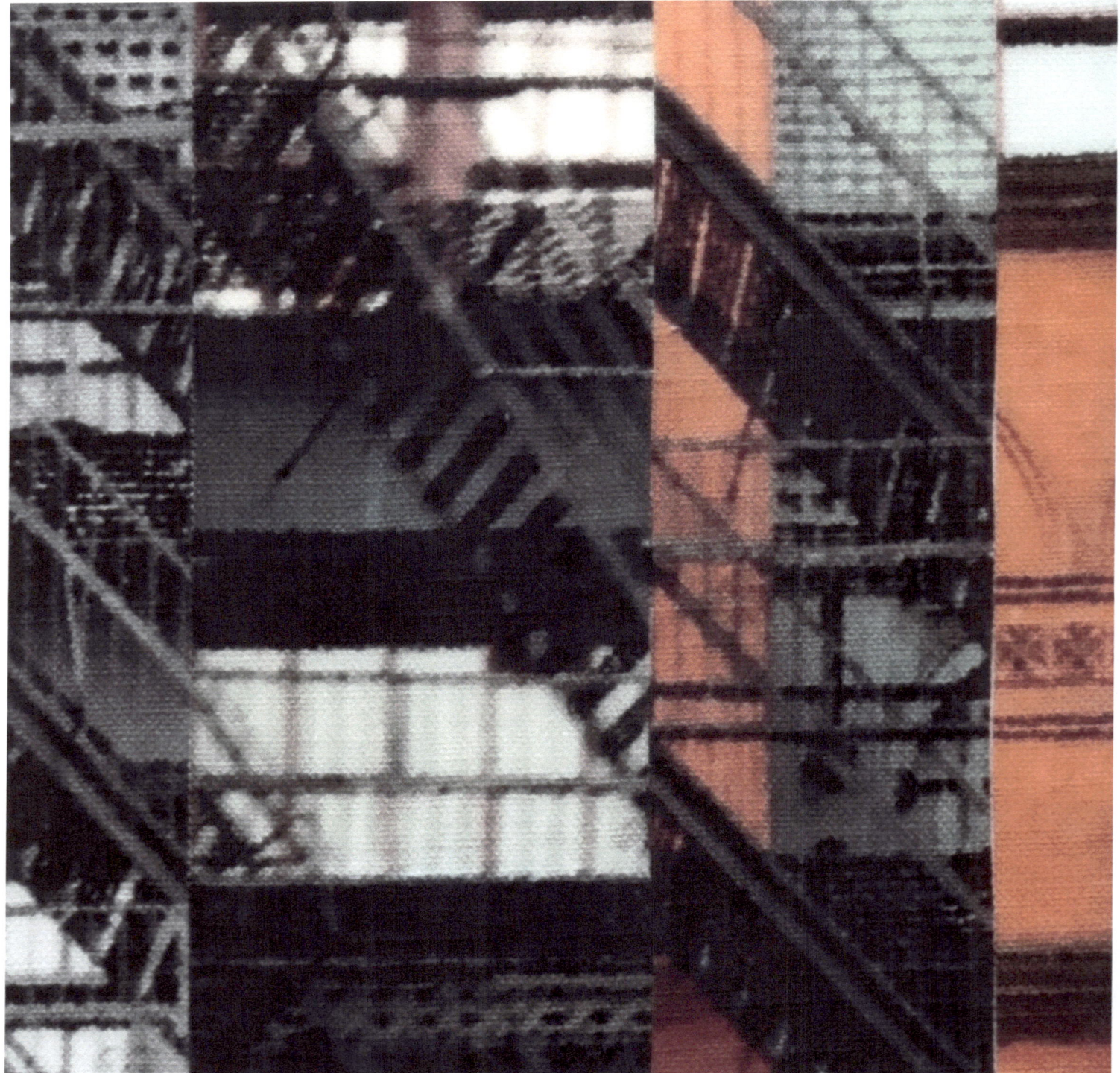

detail

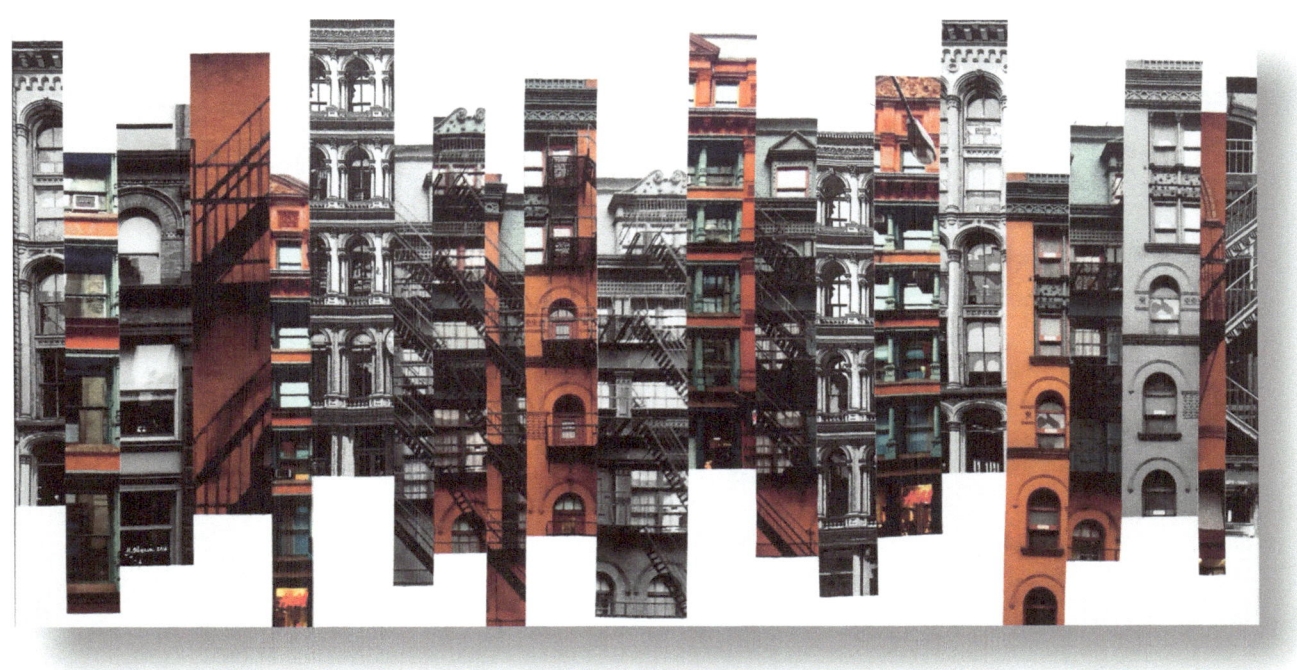

Patchwork City 68
24"x48". digitally manipulated photography, pigment printing on linen, collage on stretched canvas

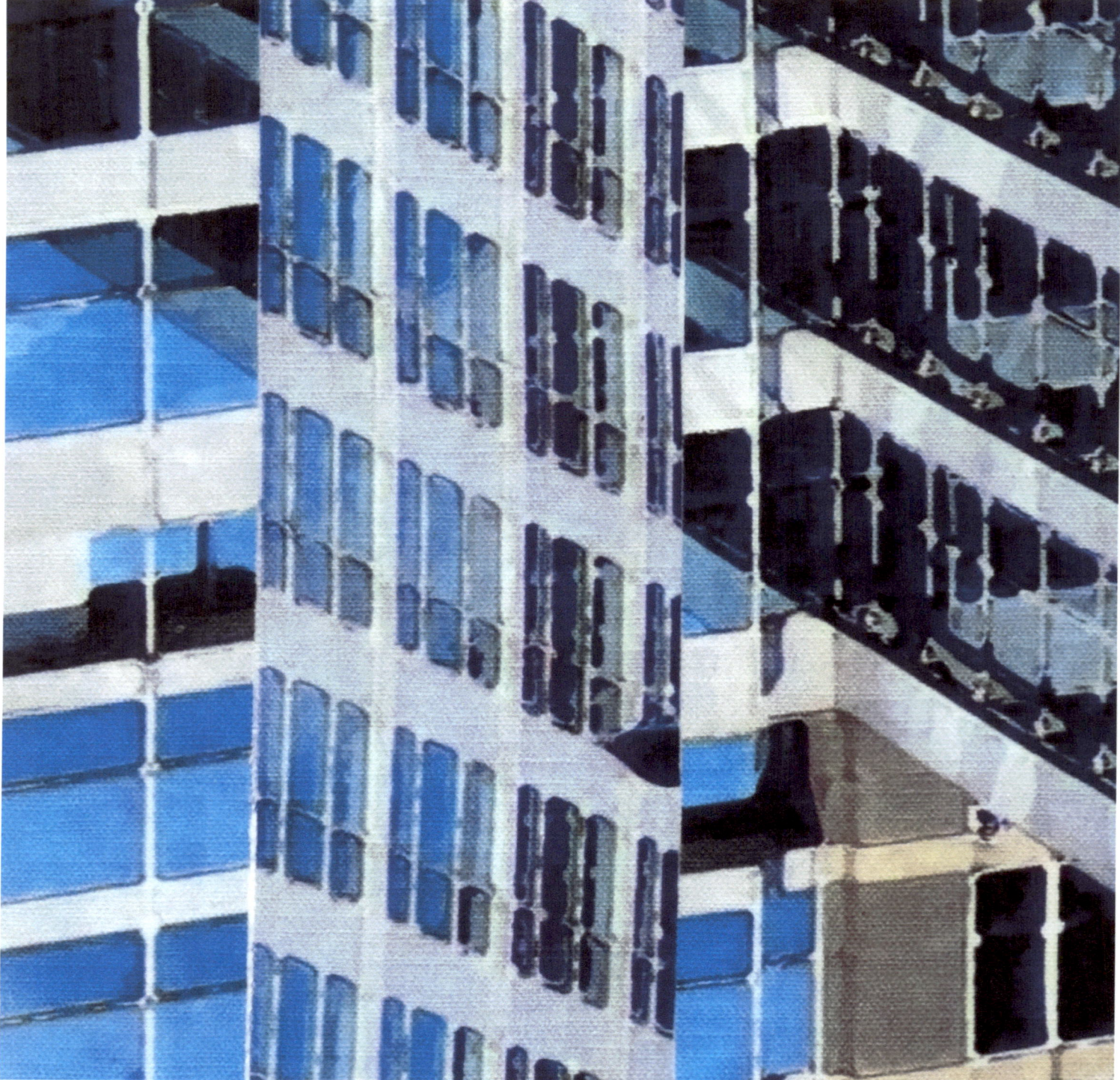

detail

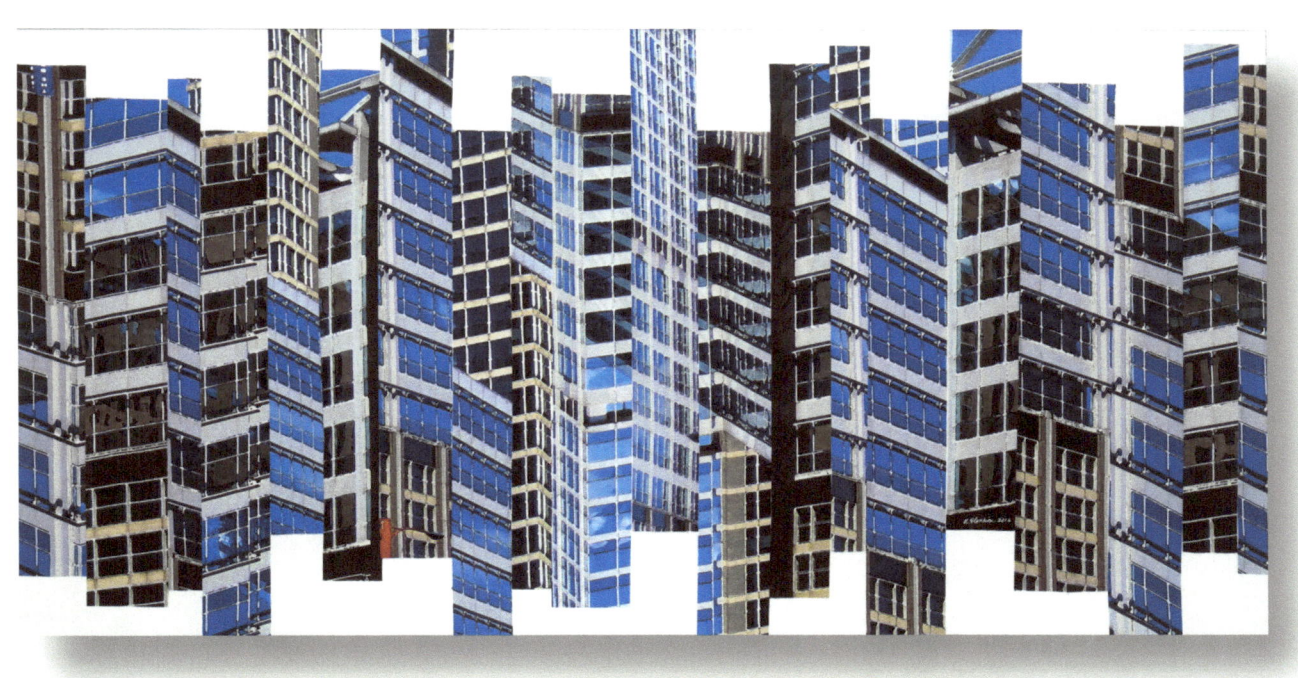

Patchwork City 67.
24"x48".   digitally manipulated photography, pigment printing on linen, collage on stretched canvas

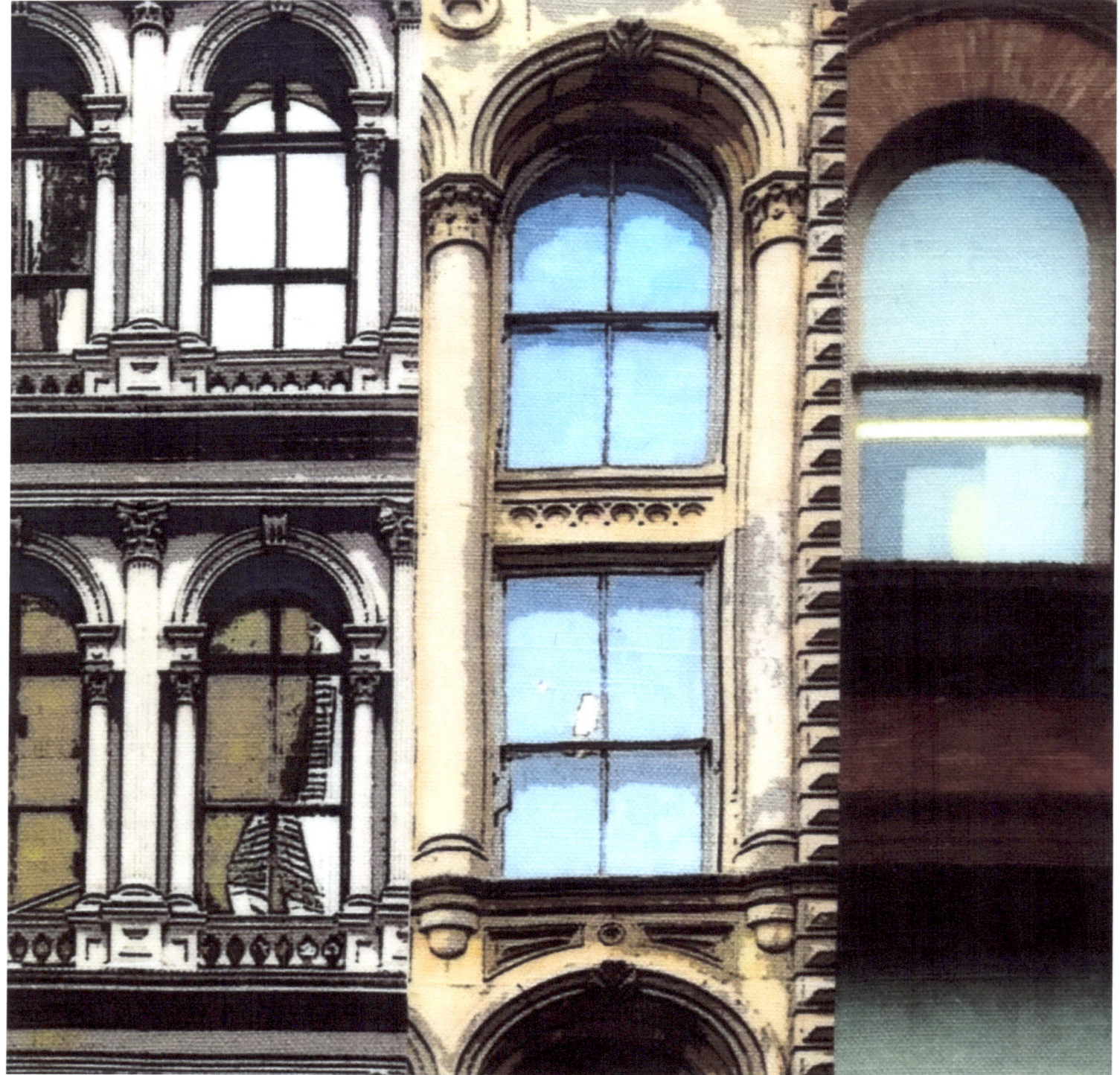

detail

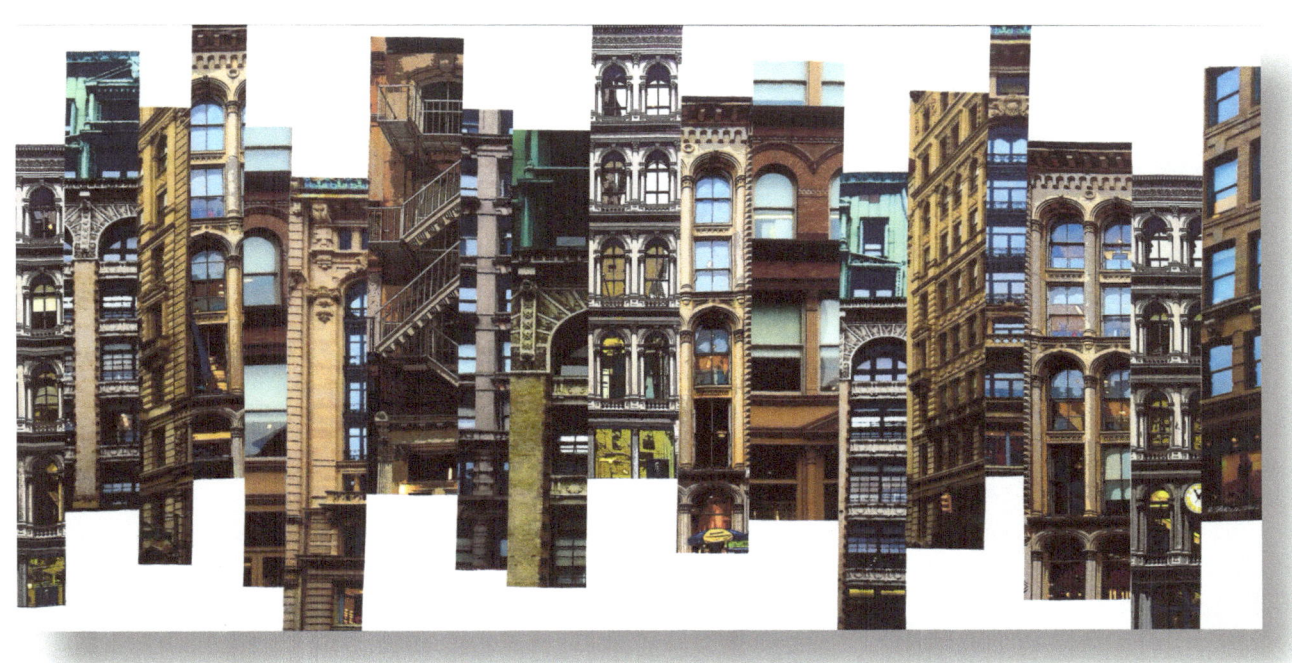

Patchwork City 66.
24"x48". digitally manipulated photography, pigment printing on linen, collage on stretched canvas

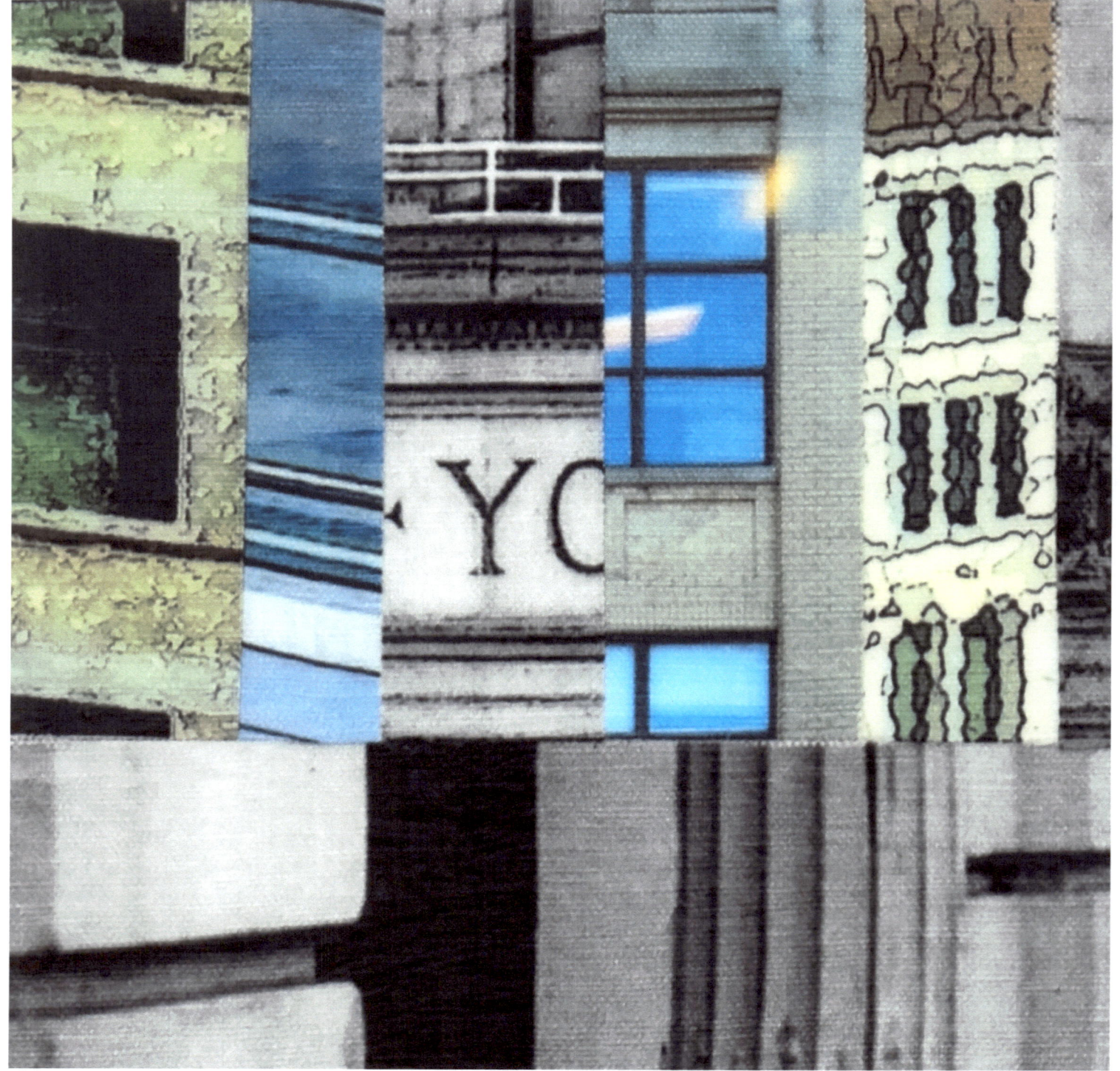

detail

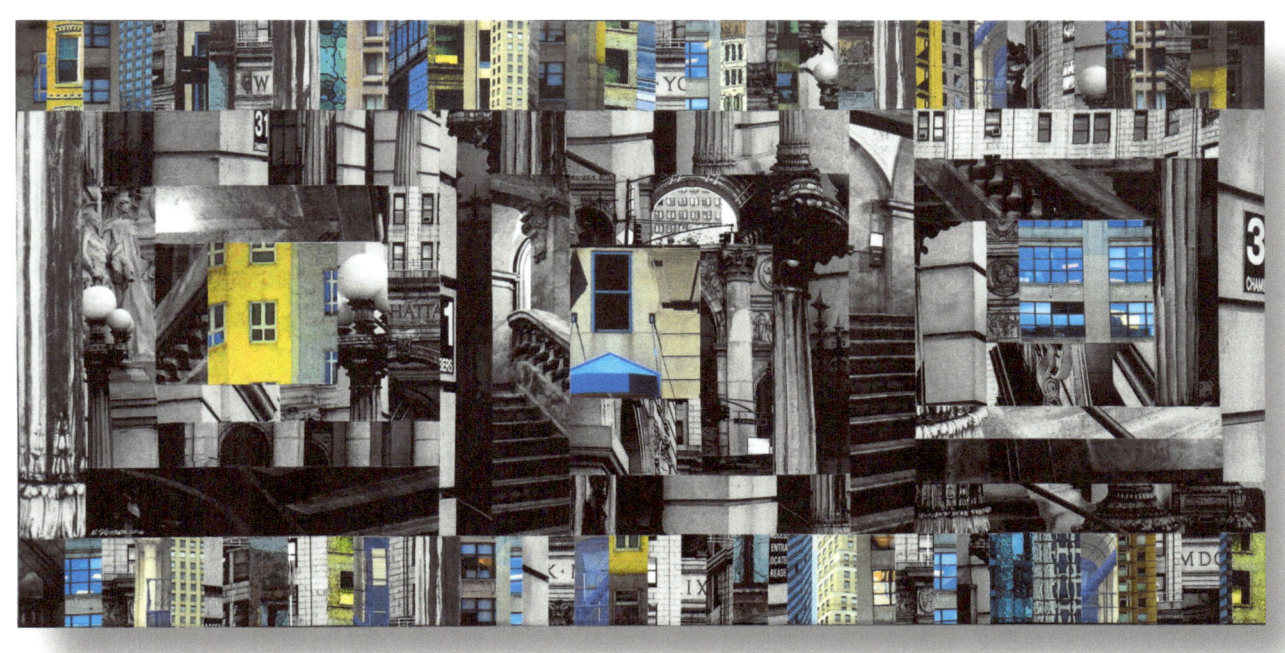

Patchwork City 64.
24"x48". digitally manipulated photography, pigment printing on linen, collage on stretched canvas

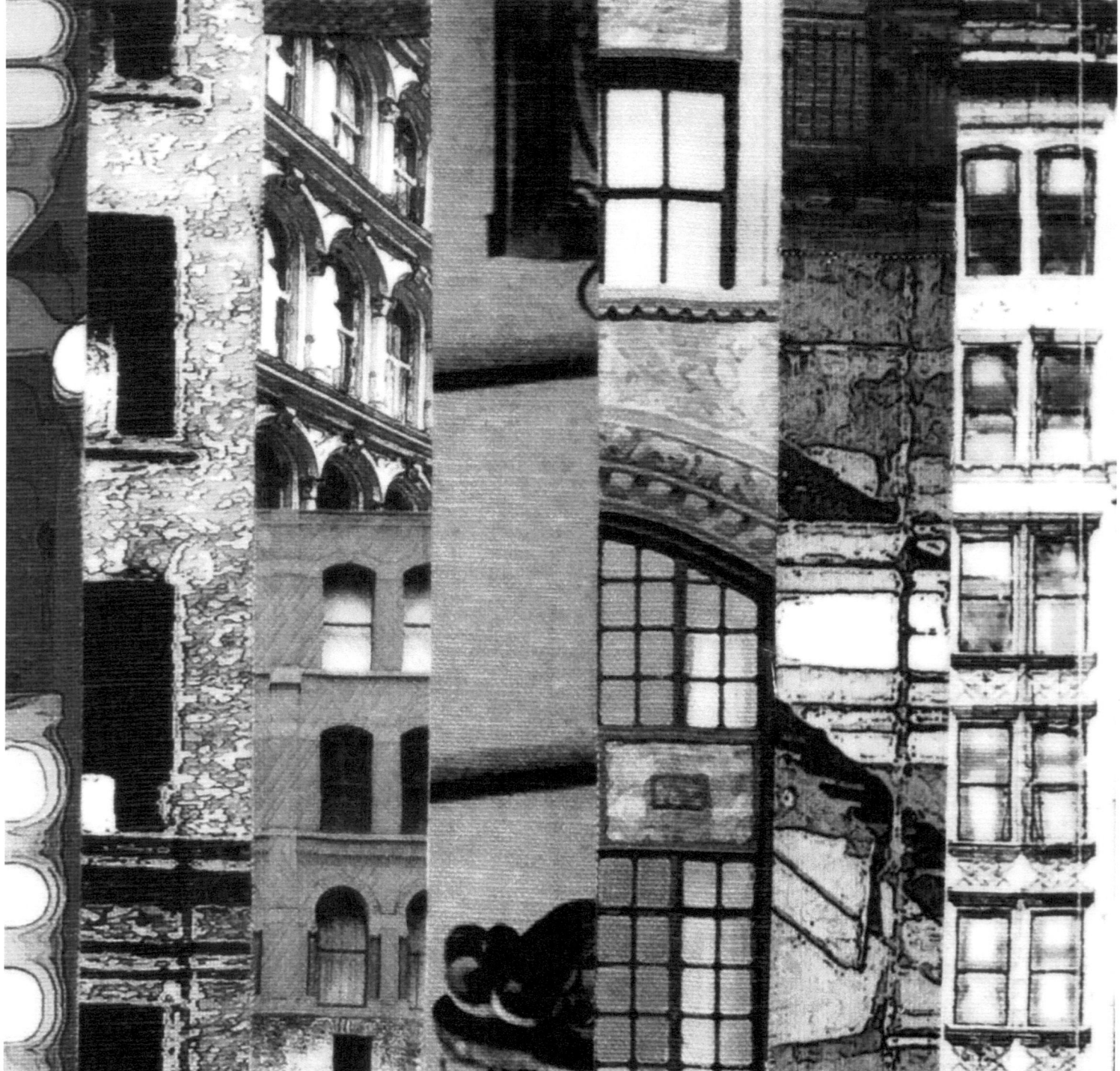

detail

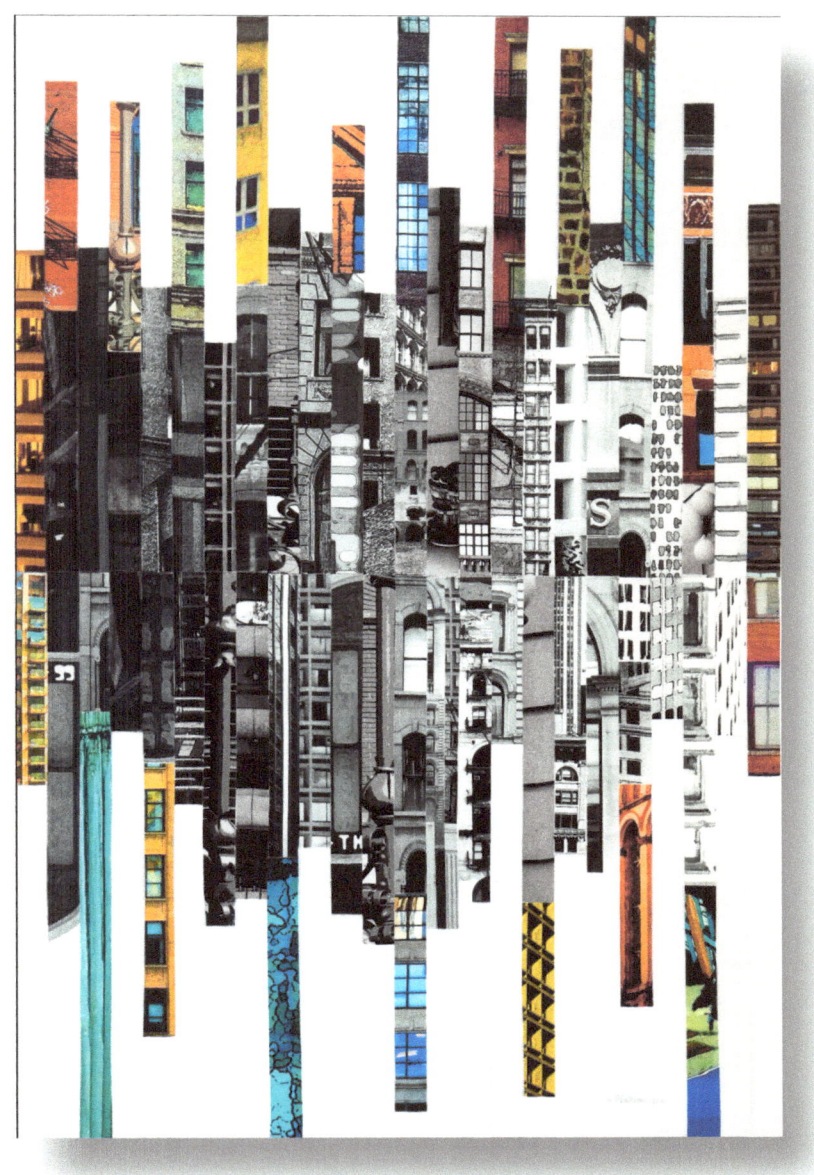

Patchwork City 65
36"x24". digitally manipulated photography, pigment printing on linen, collage on stretched canvas

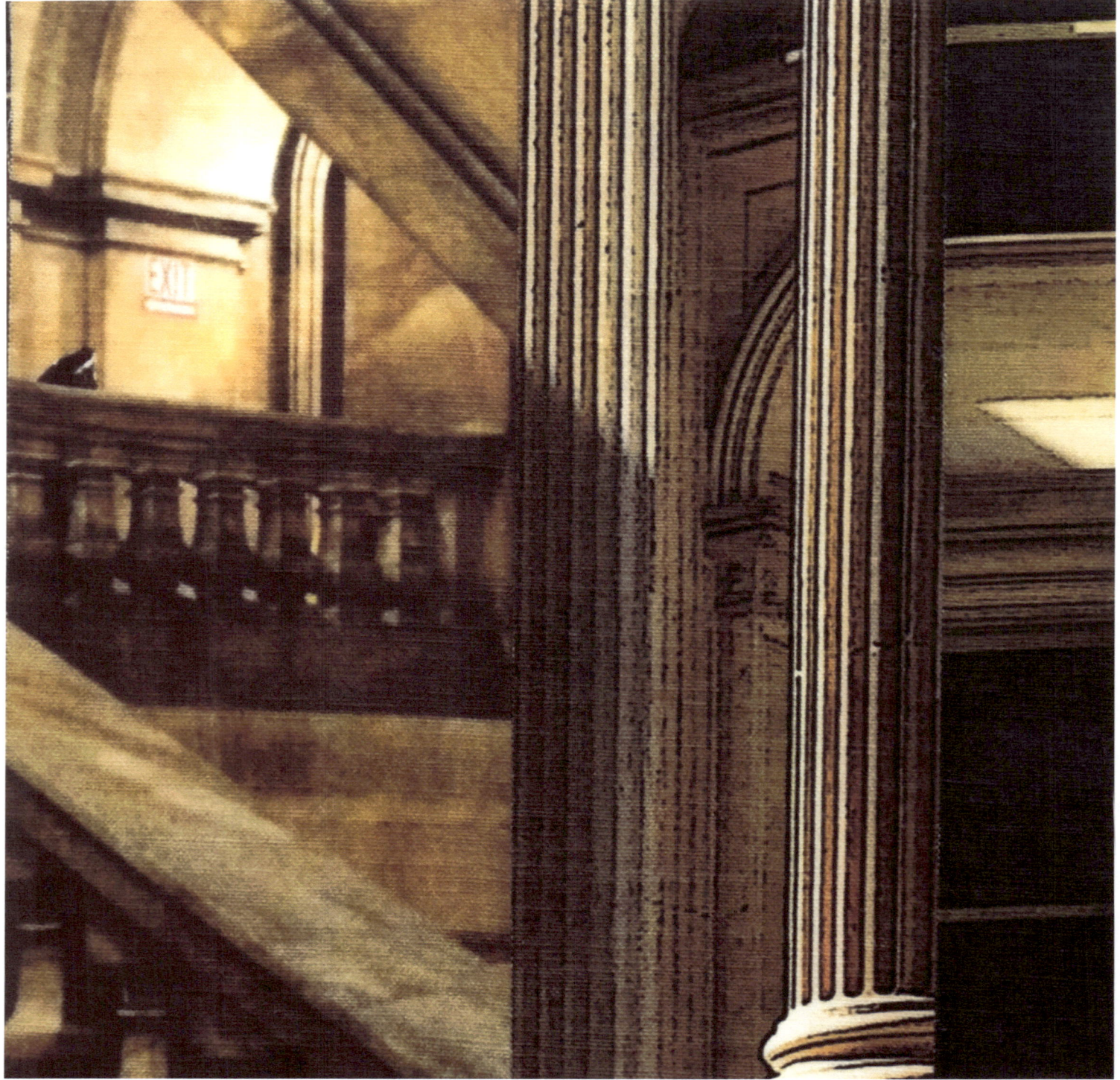

detail

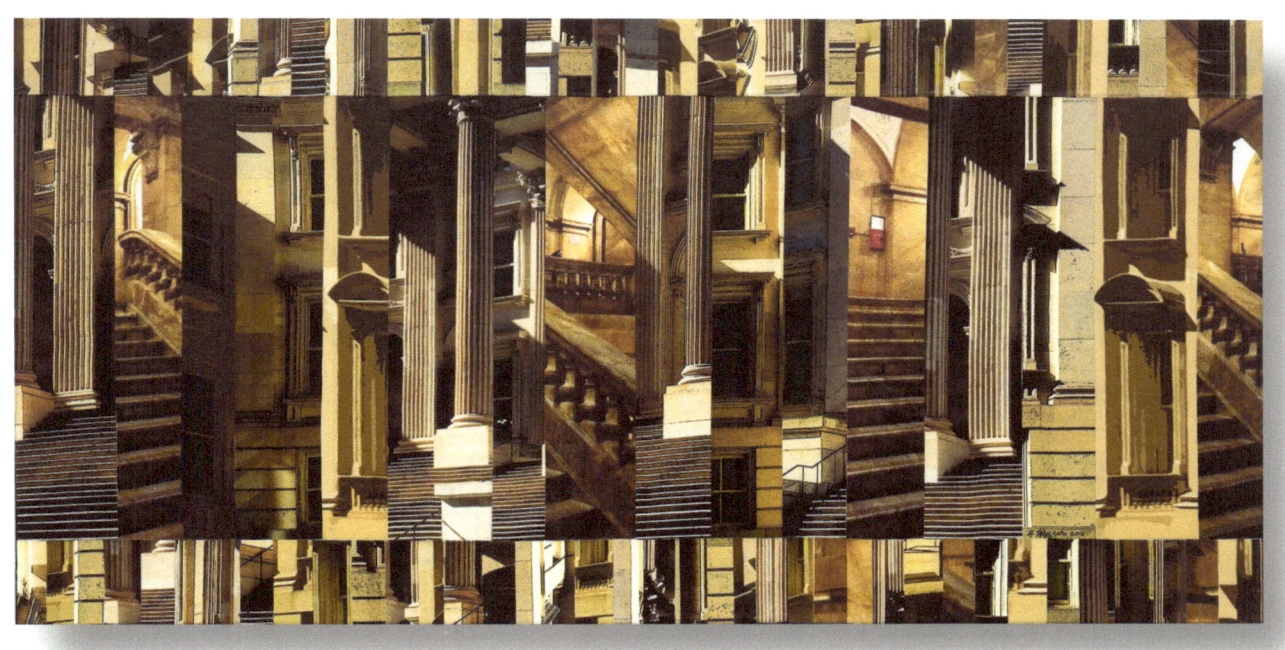

Patchwork City 63.
24"x48". digitally manipulated photography, pigment printing on linen, collage on stretched canvas

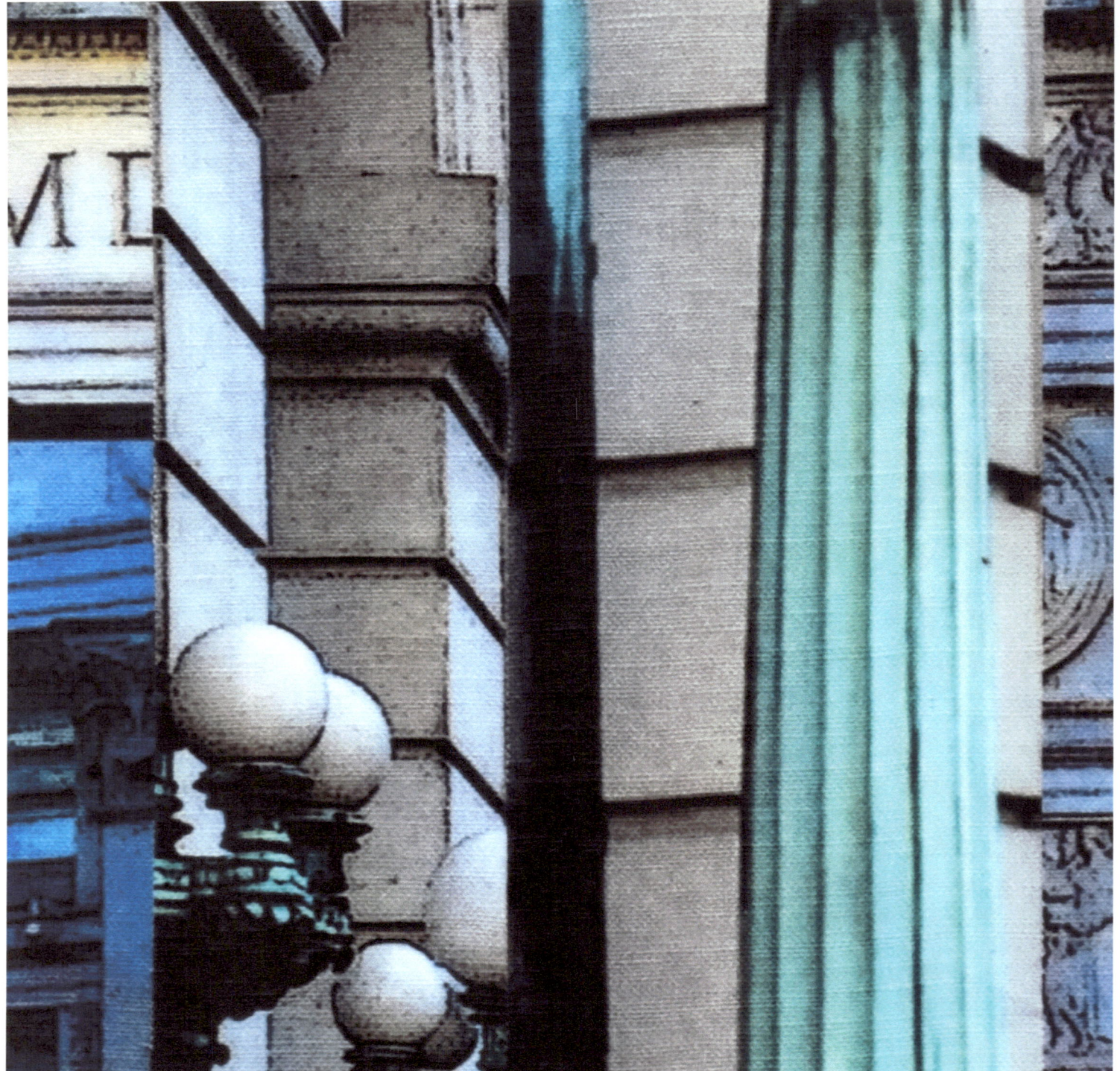

detail

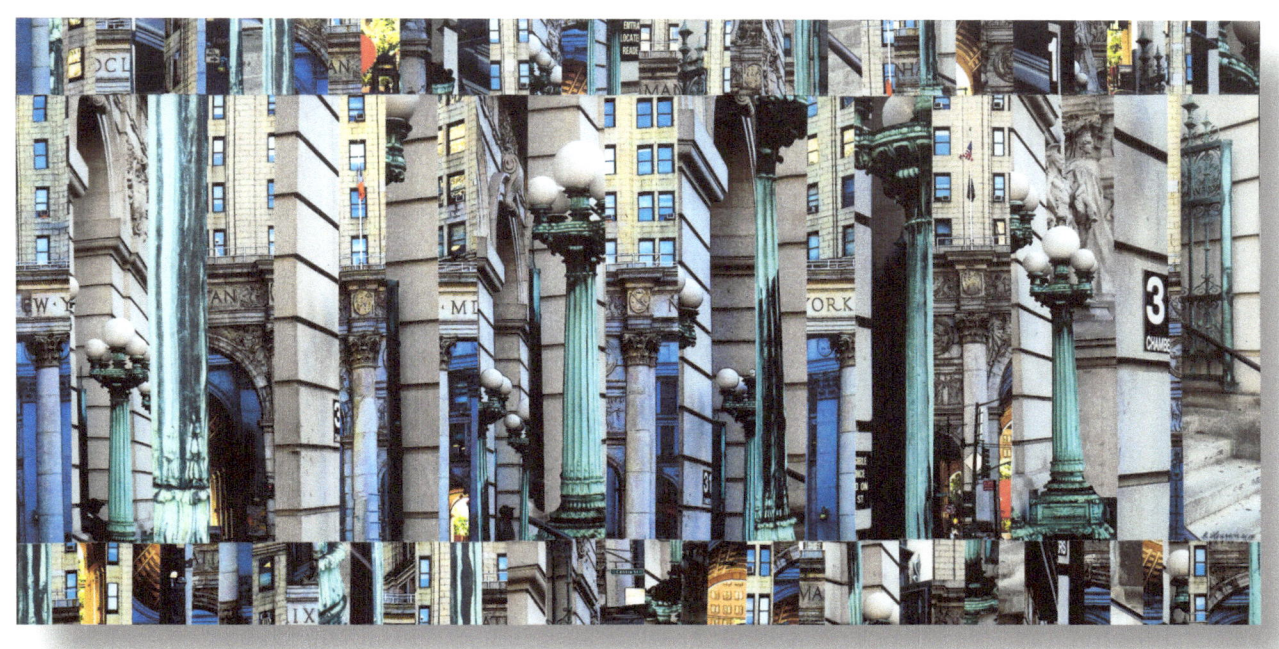

Patchwork City 62.
24"x48". digitally manipulated photography, pigment printing on linen, collage on stretched canvas

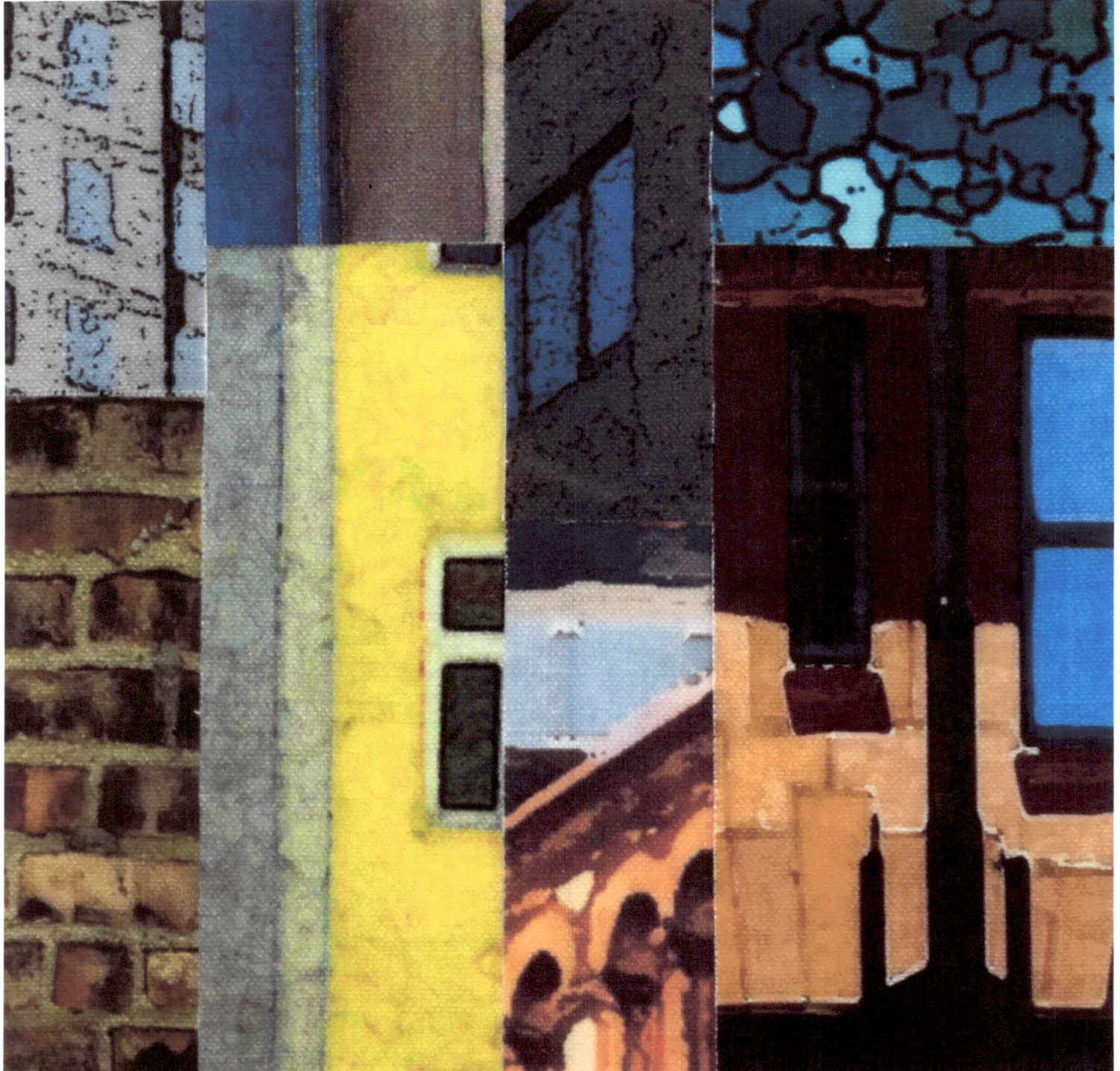

detail

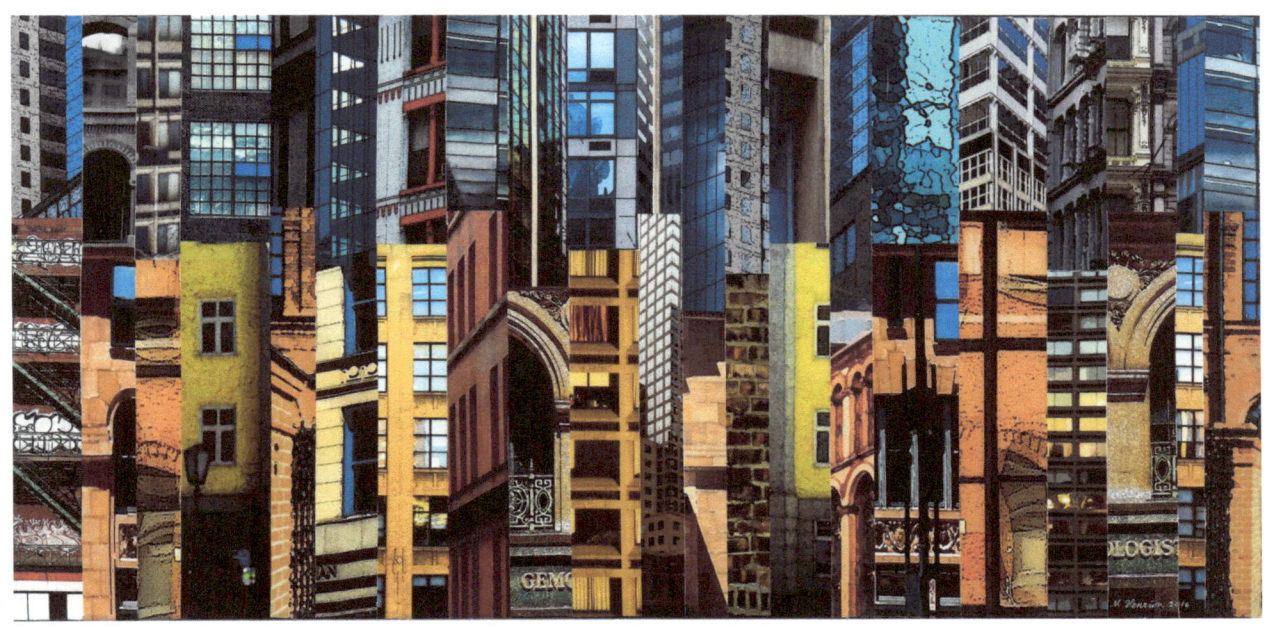

Patchwork City 61.
18"x36". digitally manipulated photography, pigment printing on linen, collage on stretched canvas

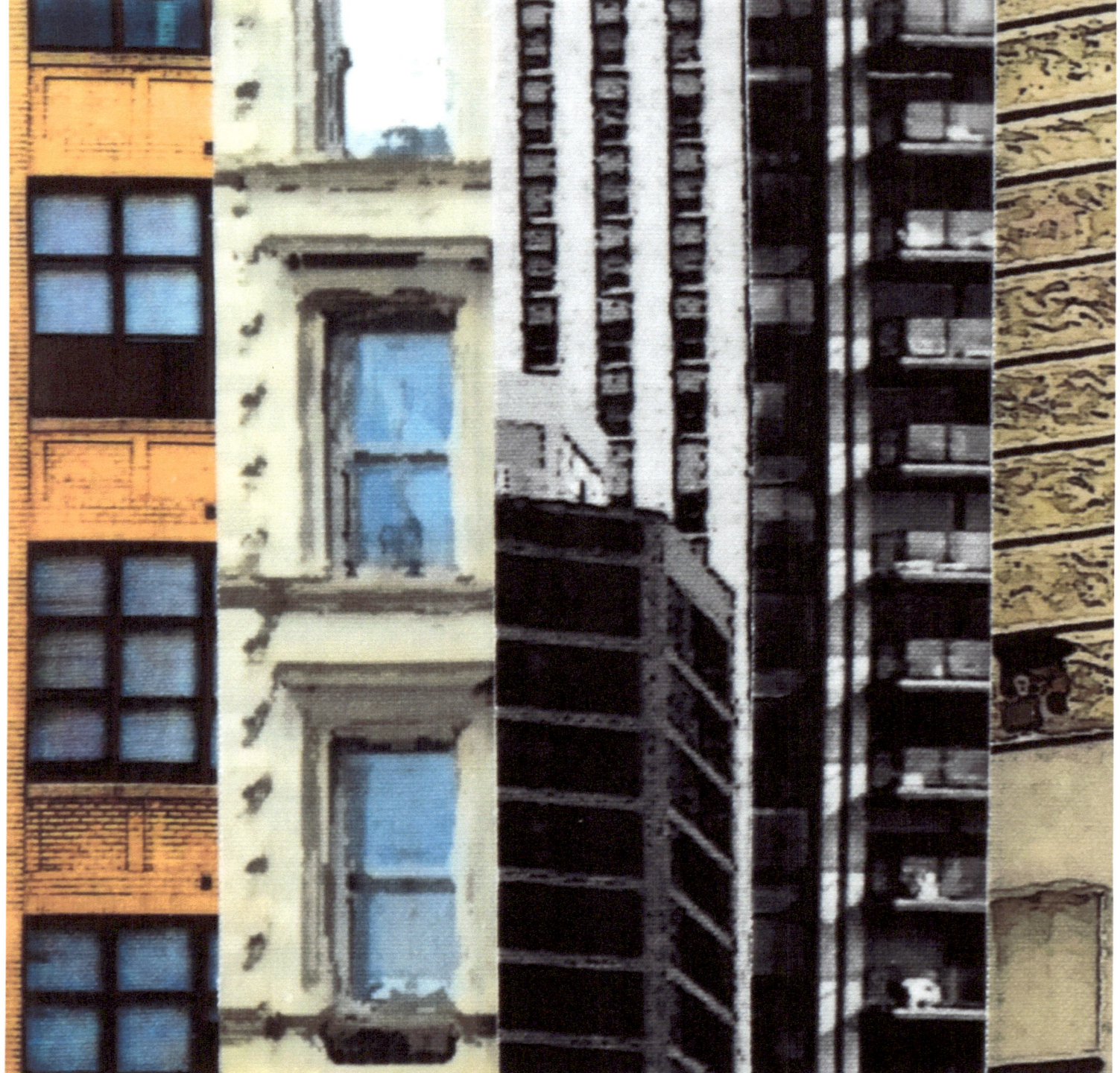

34

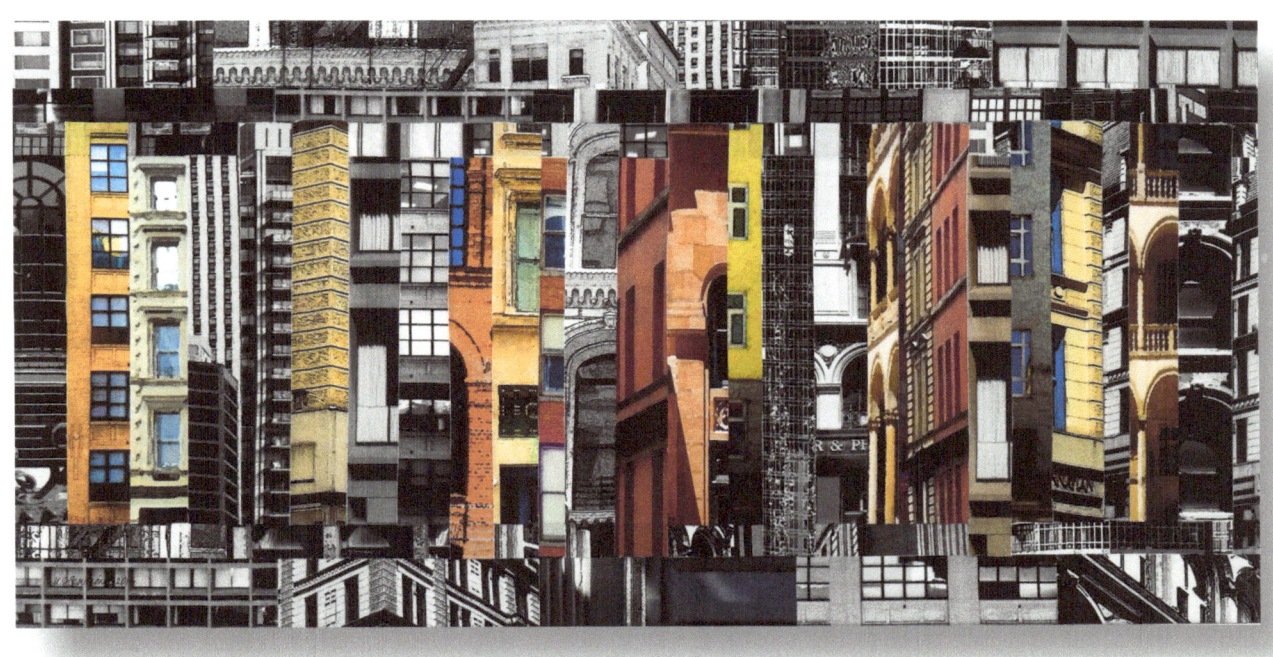

Patchwork City 60.
18"x36". digitally manipulated photography, pigment printing on linen, collage on stretched canvas

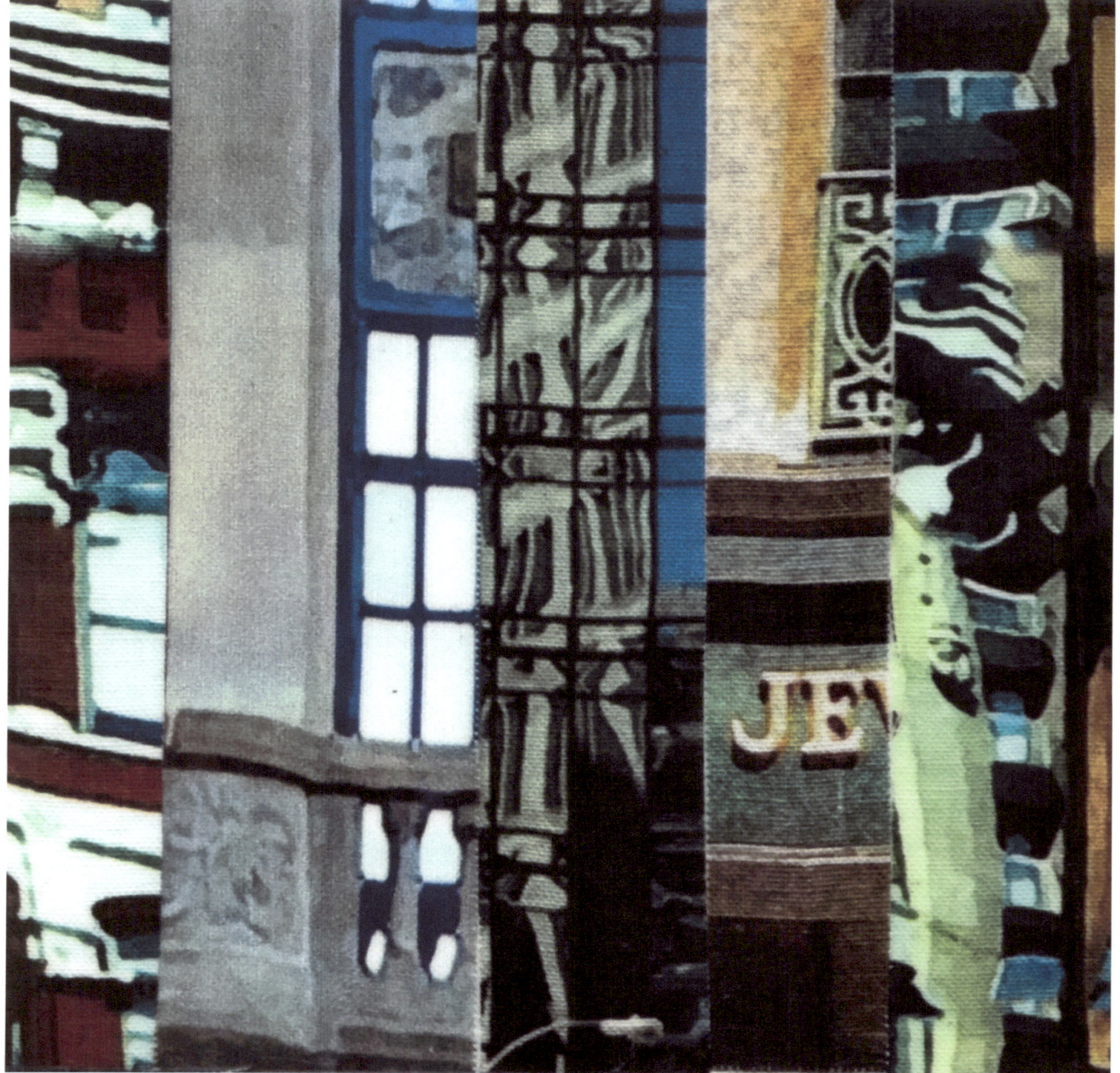

detail

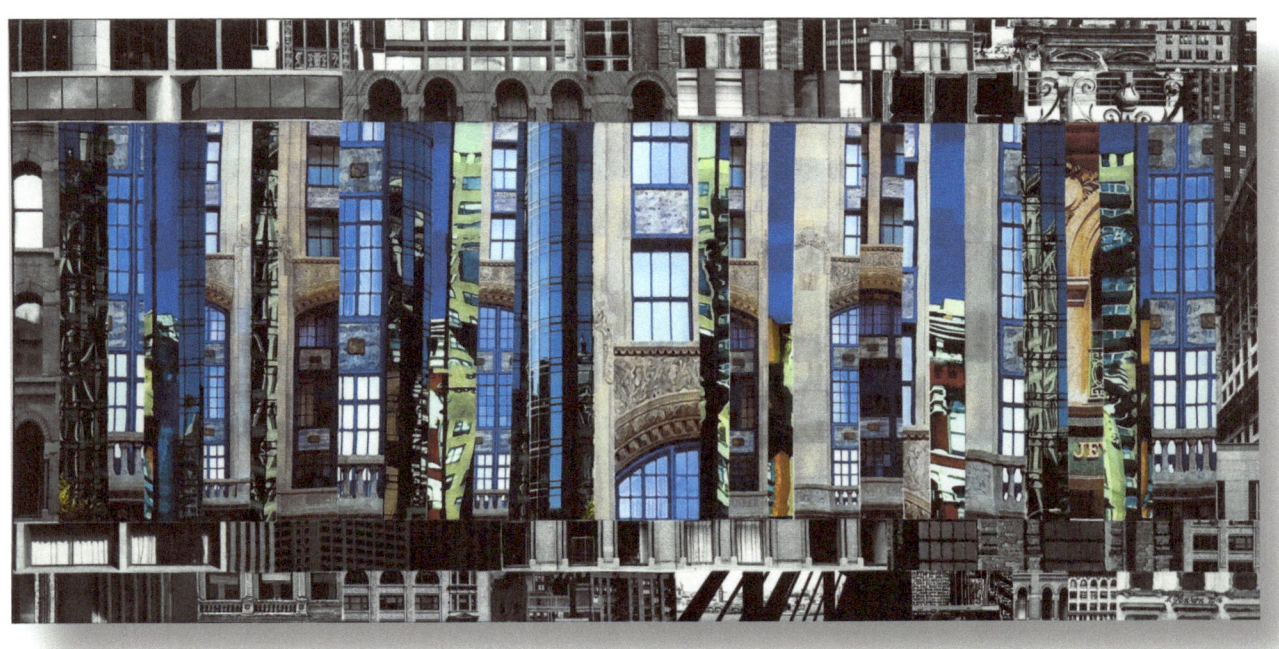

Patchwork City 59.
18"x36" digitally manipulated photography, pigment printing on linen, collage on stretched canvas

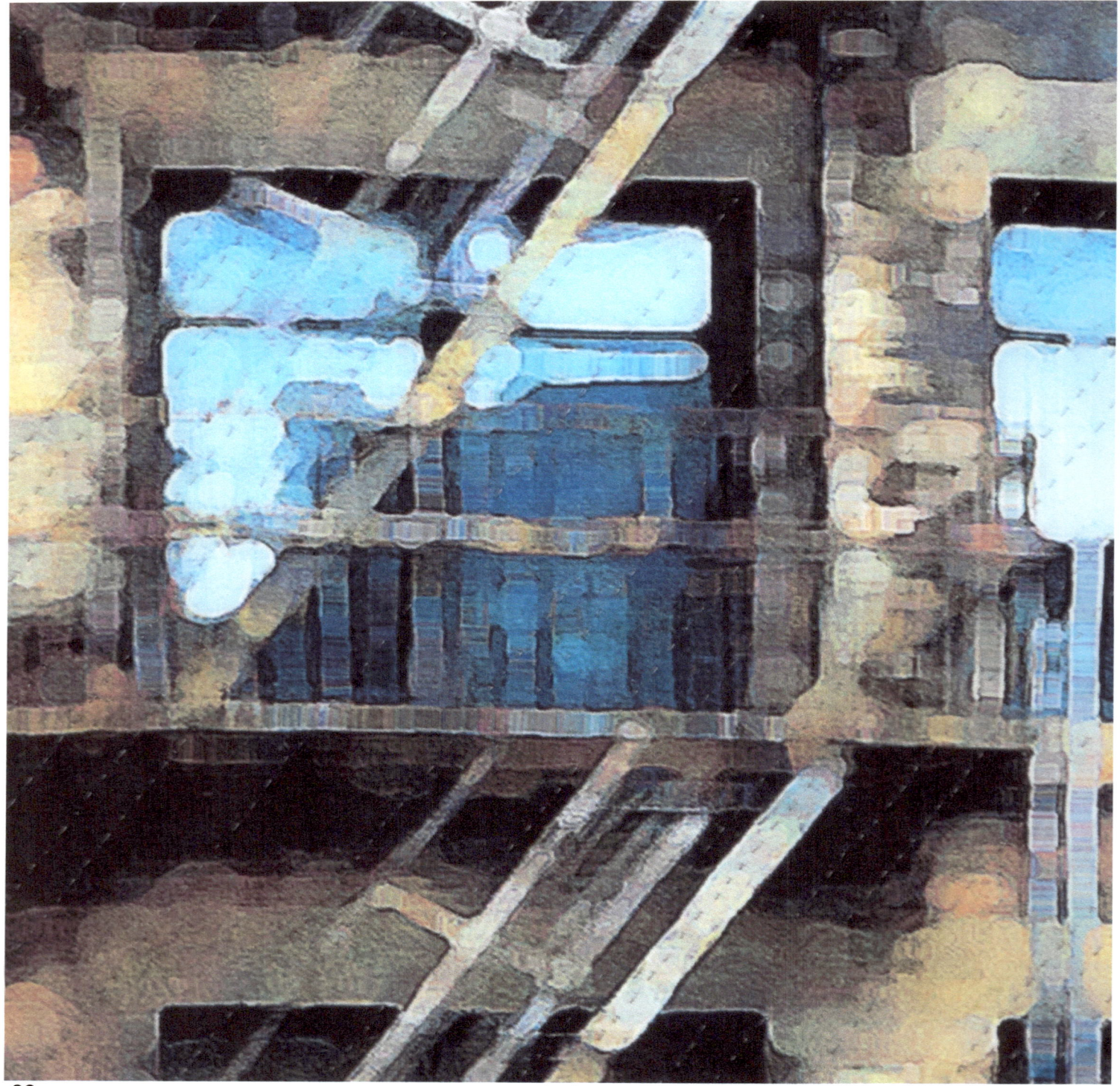

detail

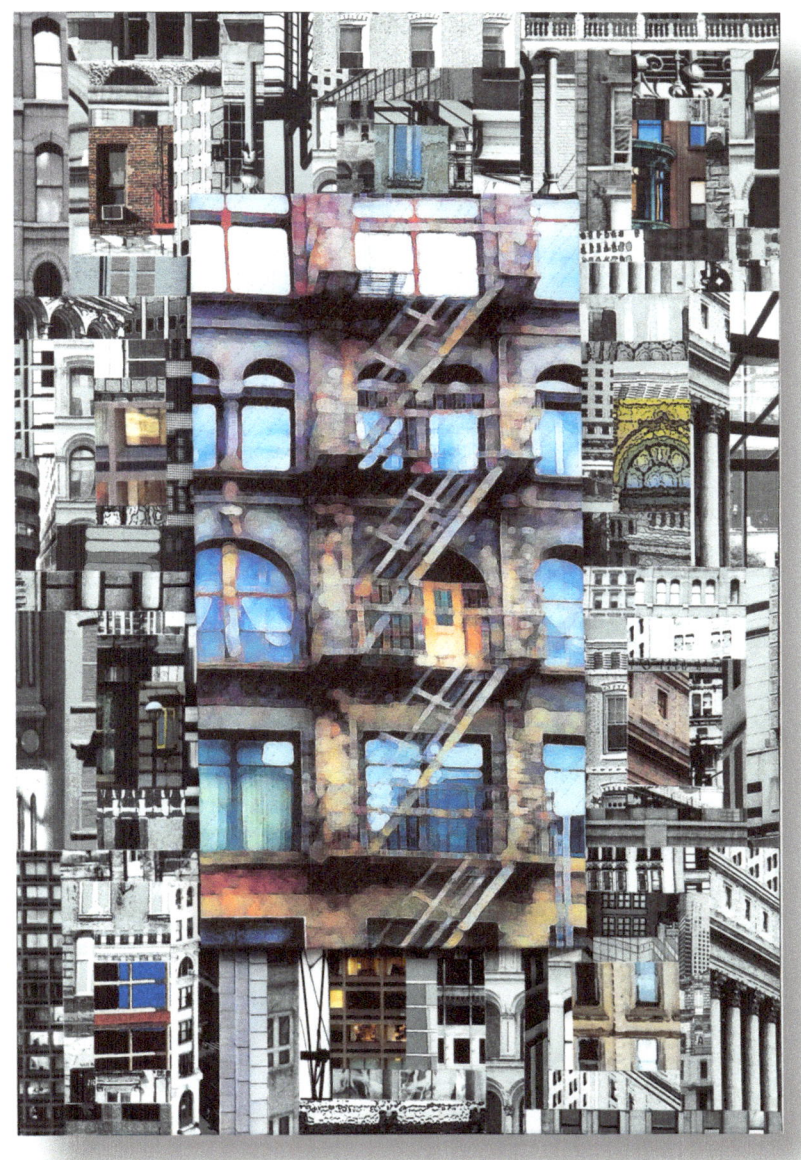

Patchwork City 29
36"x24". digitally manipulated photography, pigment printing on linen and silk, hand quilting, collage on stretched canvas

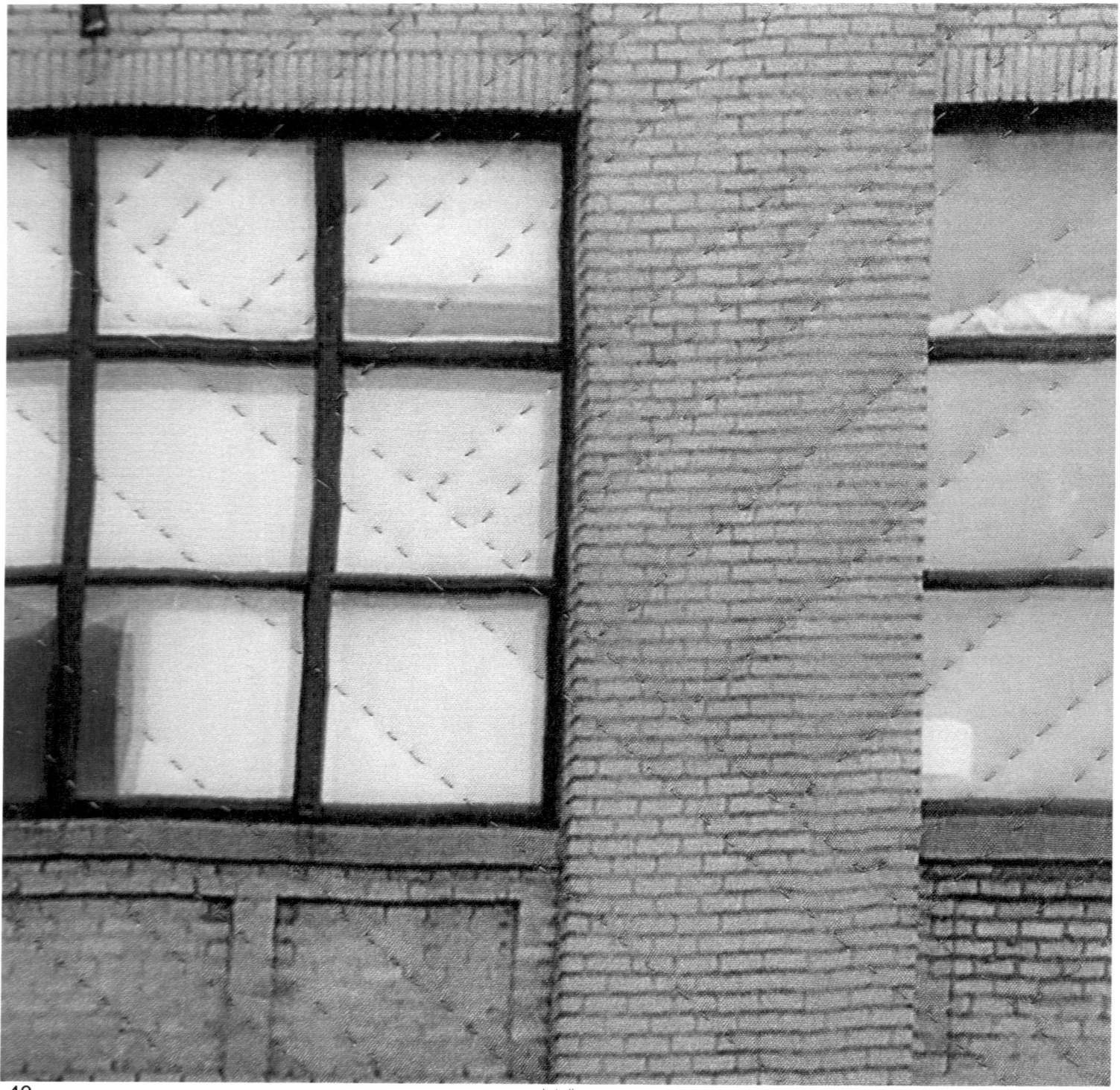

detail

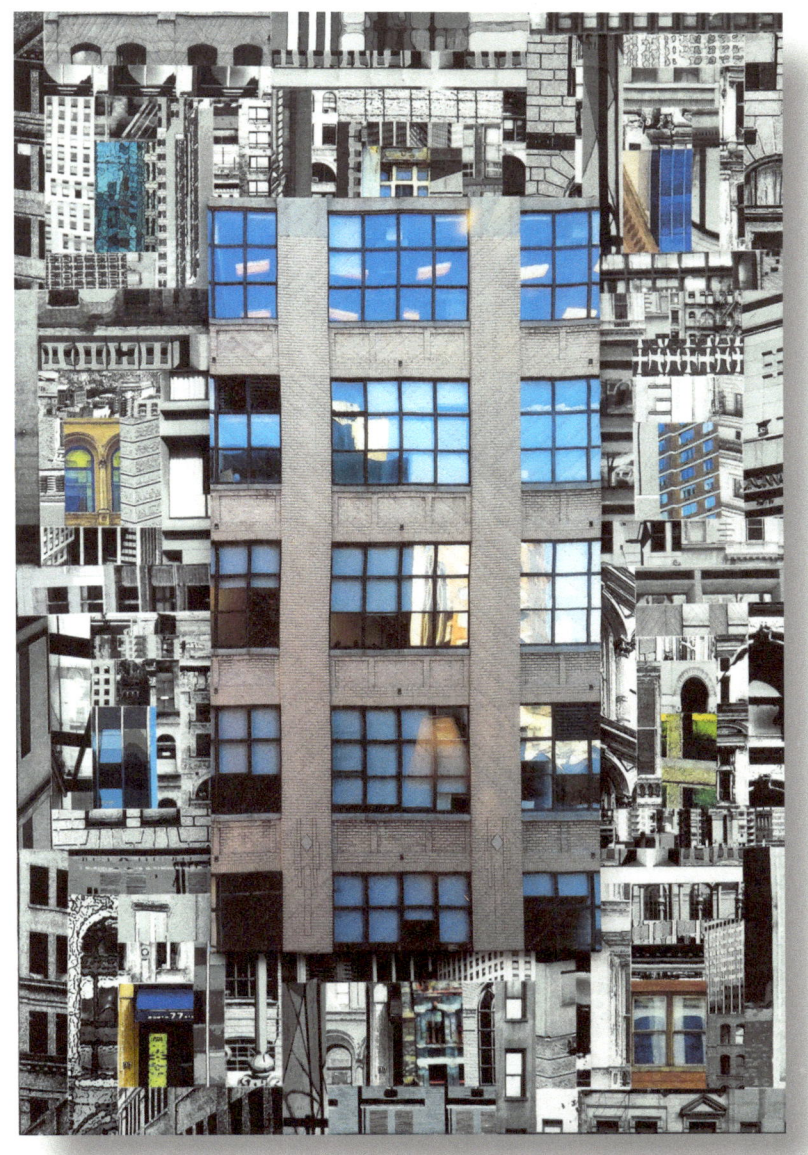

Patchwork City 28
36"x24". digitally manipulated photography, pigment printing on linen and silk, hand quilting, collage on stretched canvas

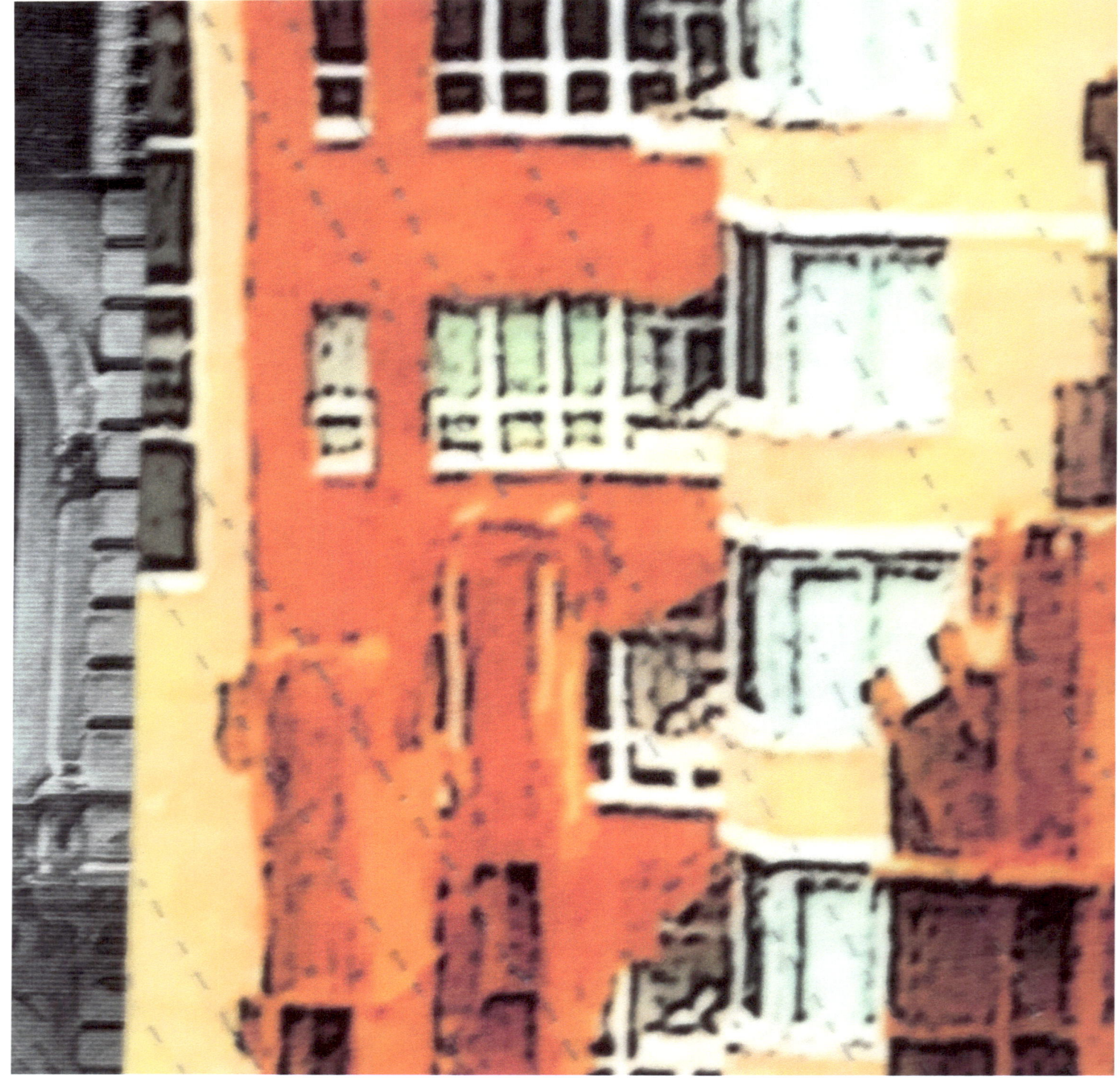

detail

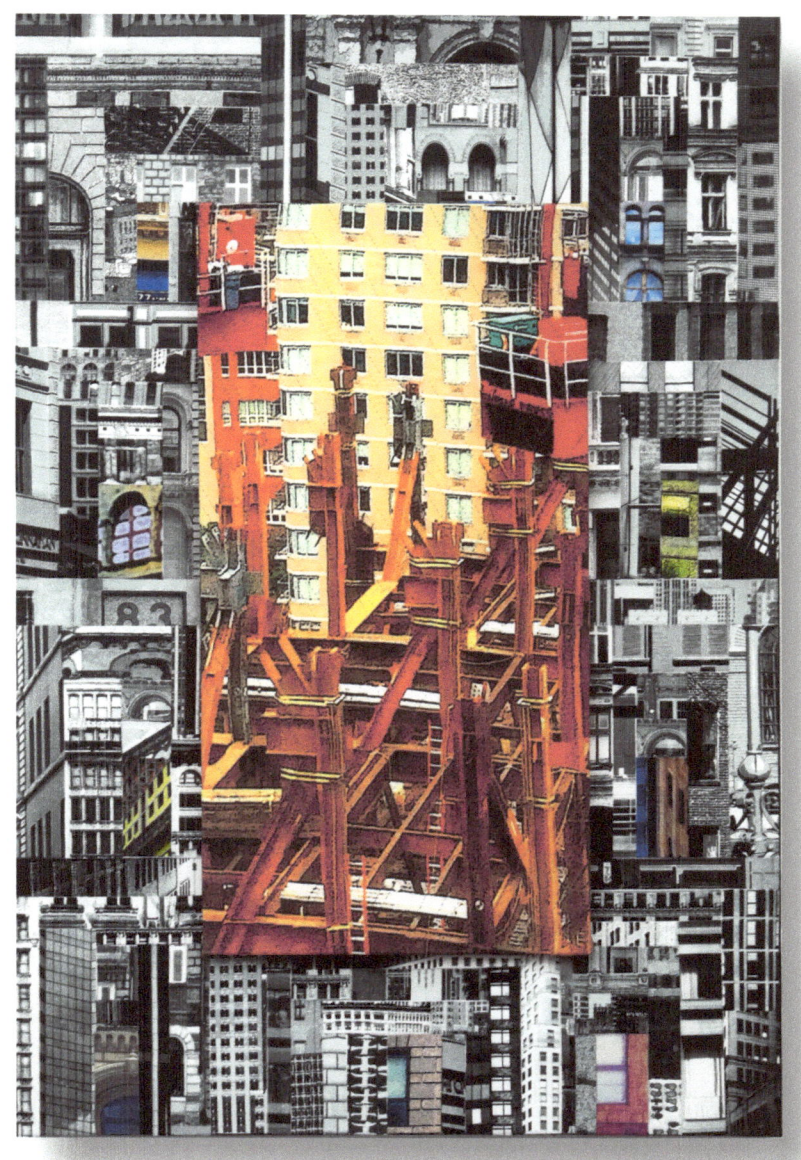

Patchwork City 27.
36"x24". digitally manipulated photography, pigment printing on linen and silk, hand quilting, collage on stretched canvas

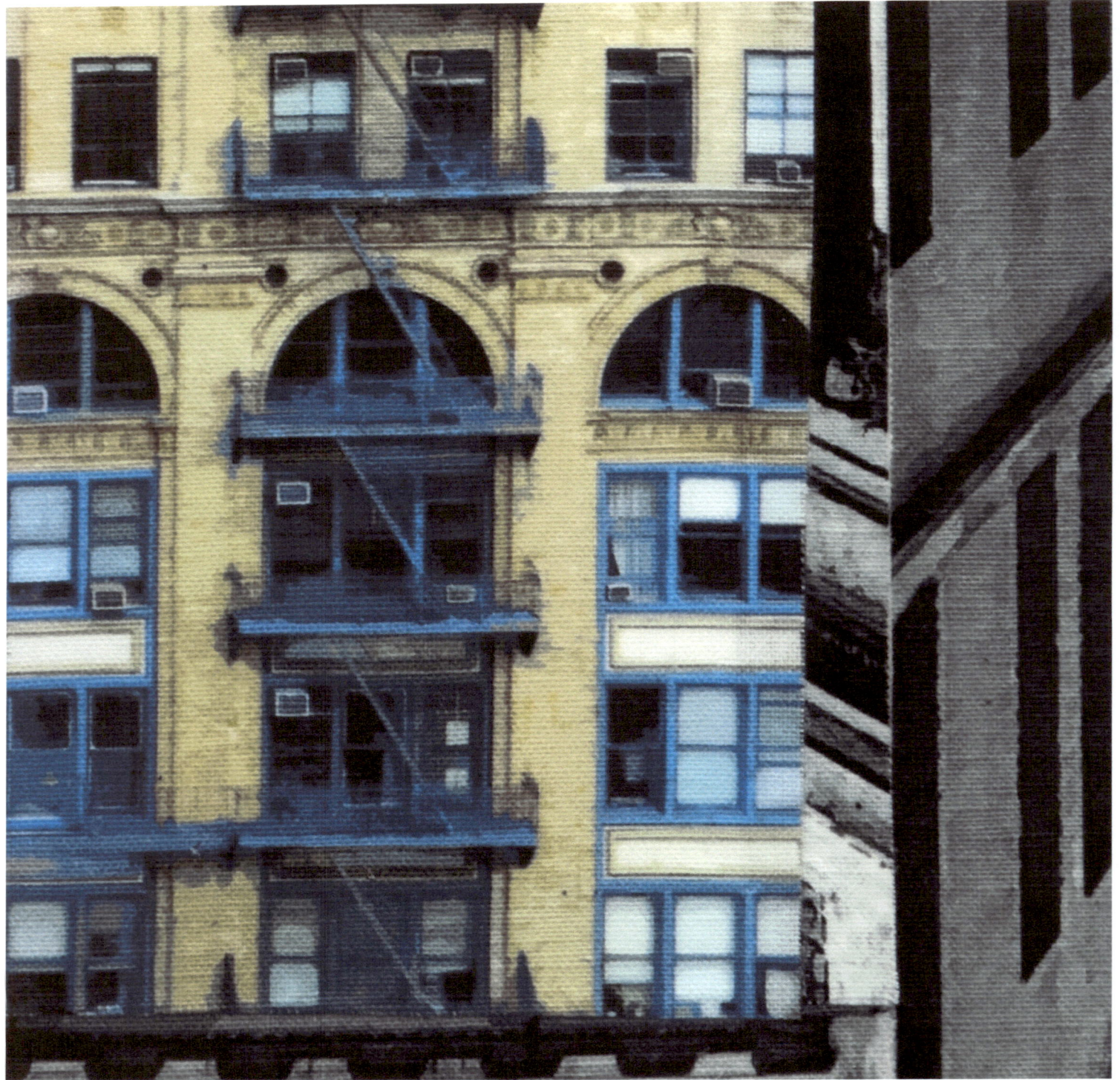

detail

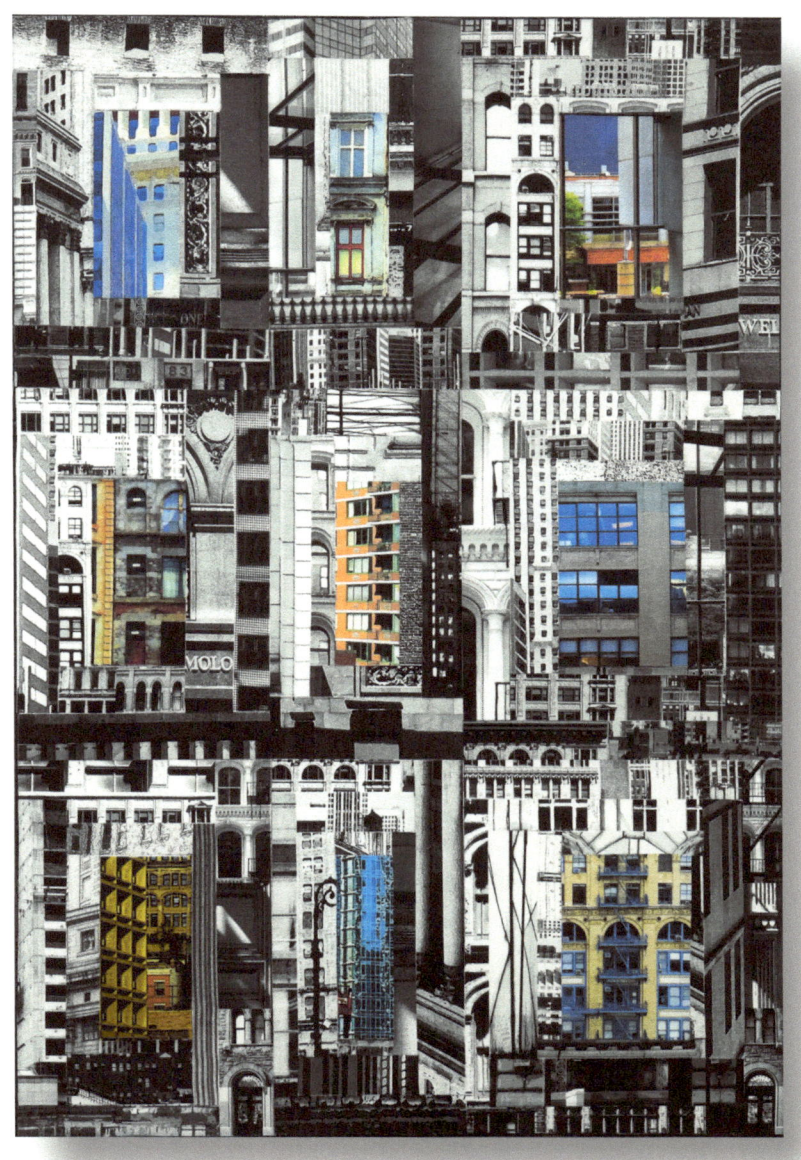

Patchwork City 26.
36"x24"   digitally manipulated photography, pigment printing on linen, collage on stretched canvas

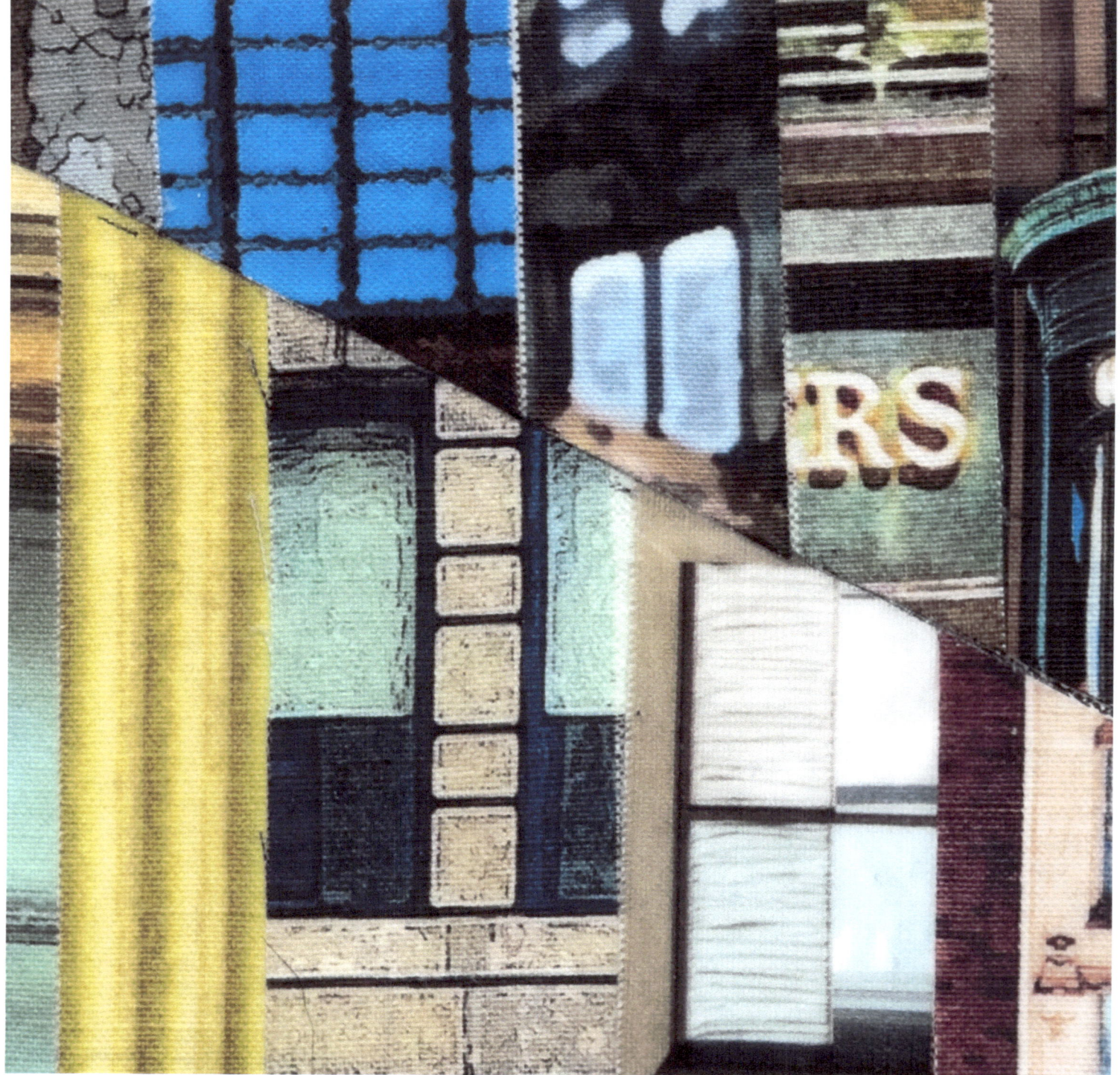

46

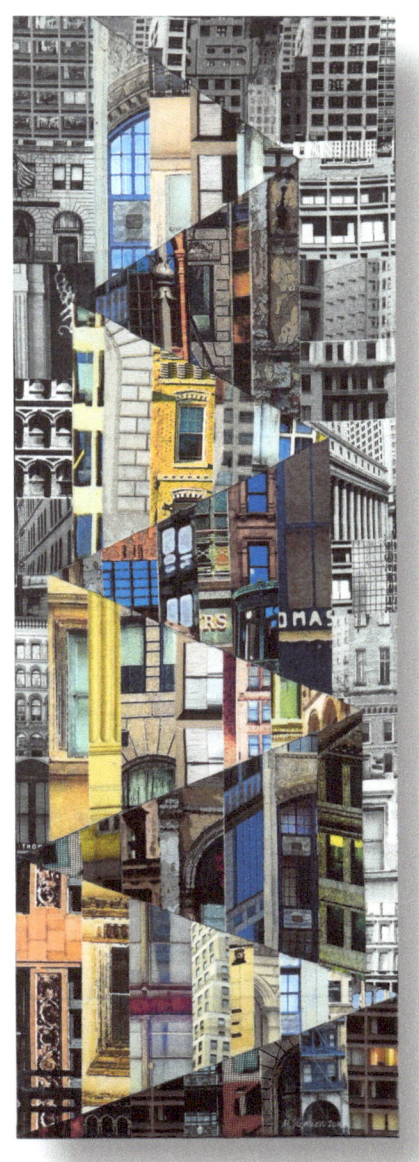

Patchwork City 25.
36"x12"". digitally manipulated photography, pigment printing on linen, collage on stretched canvas

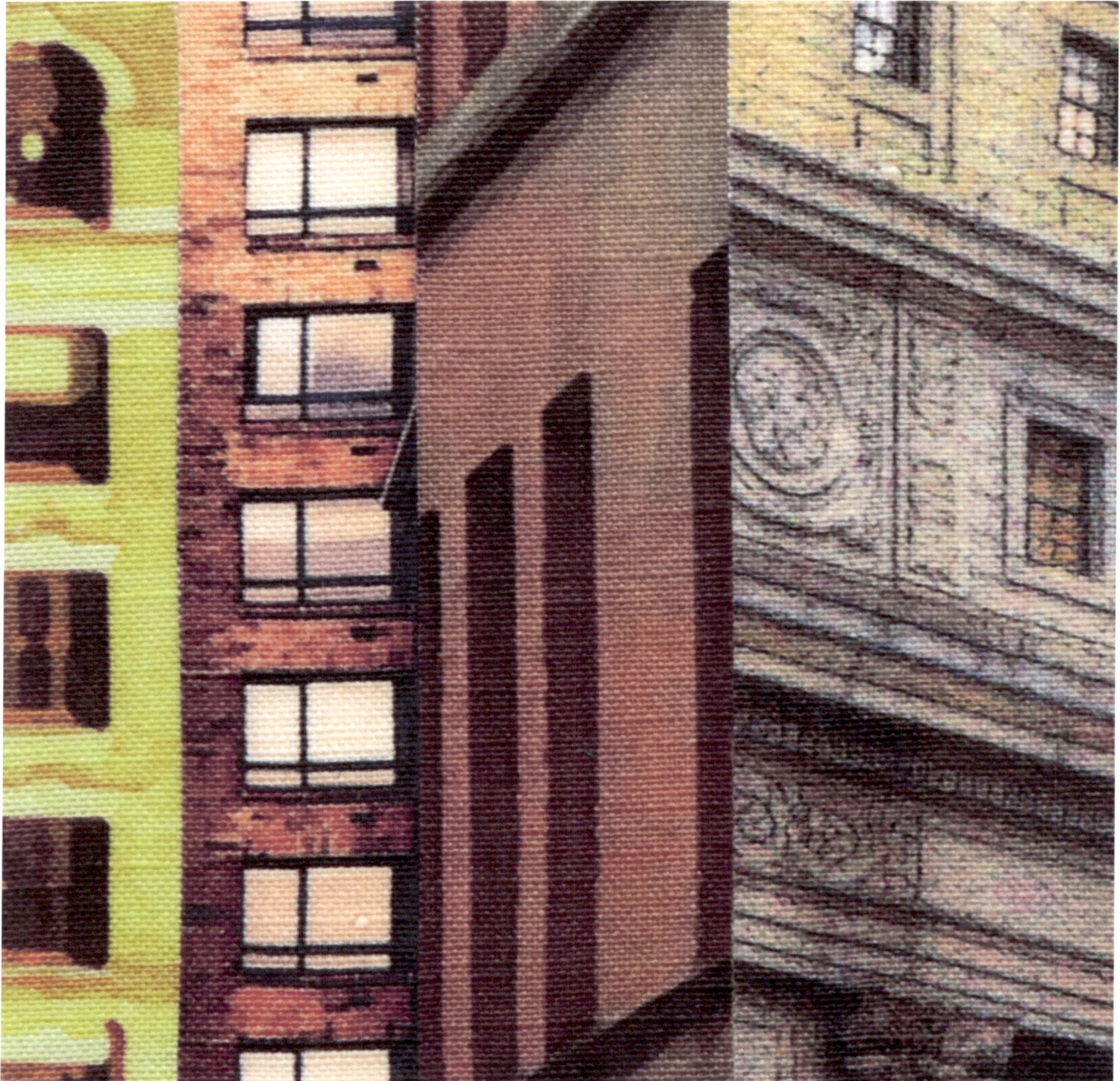

48

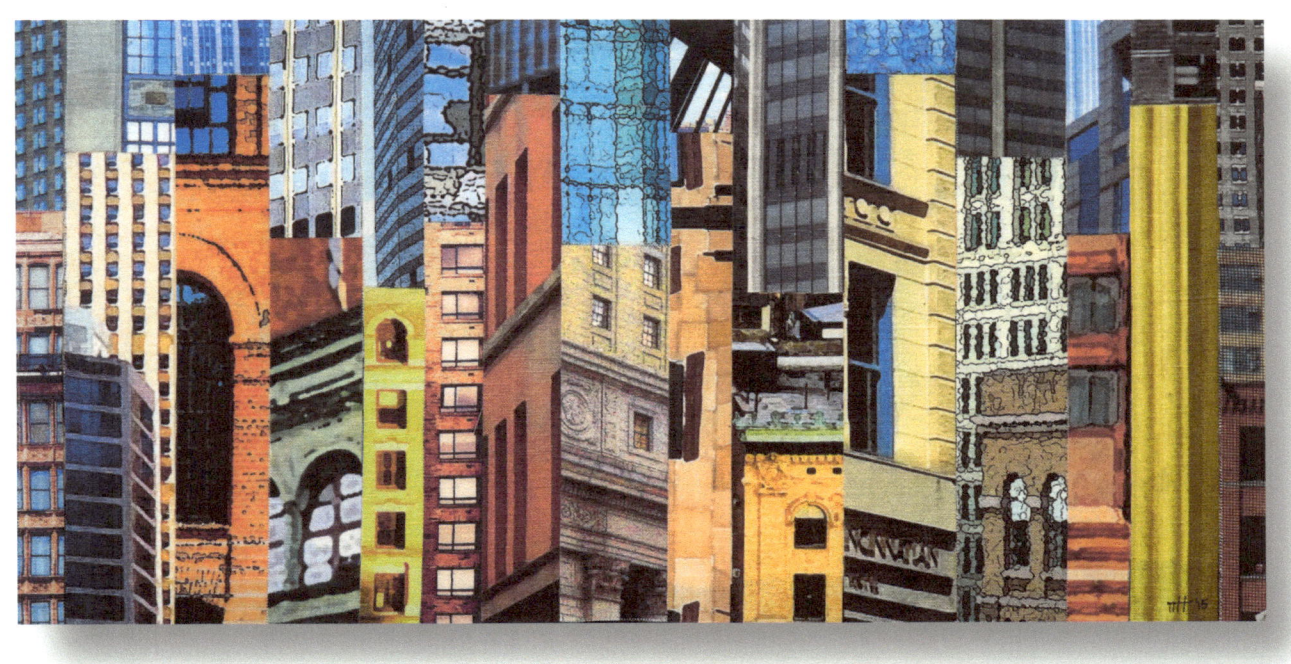

Patchwork City 20.
10"x20". digitally manipulated photography, pigment printing on linen, collage on wood panel

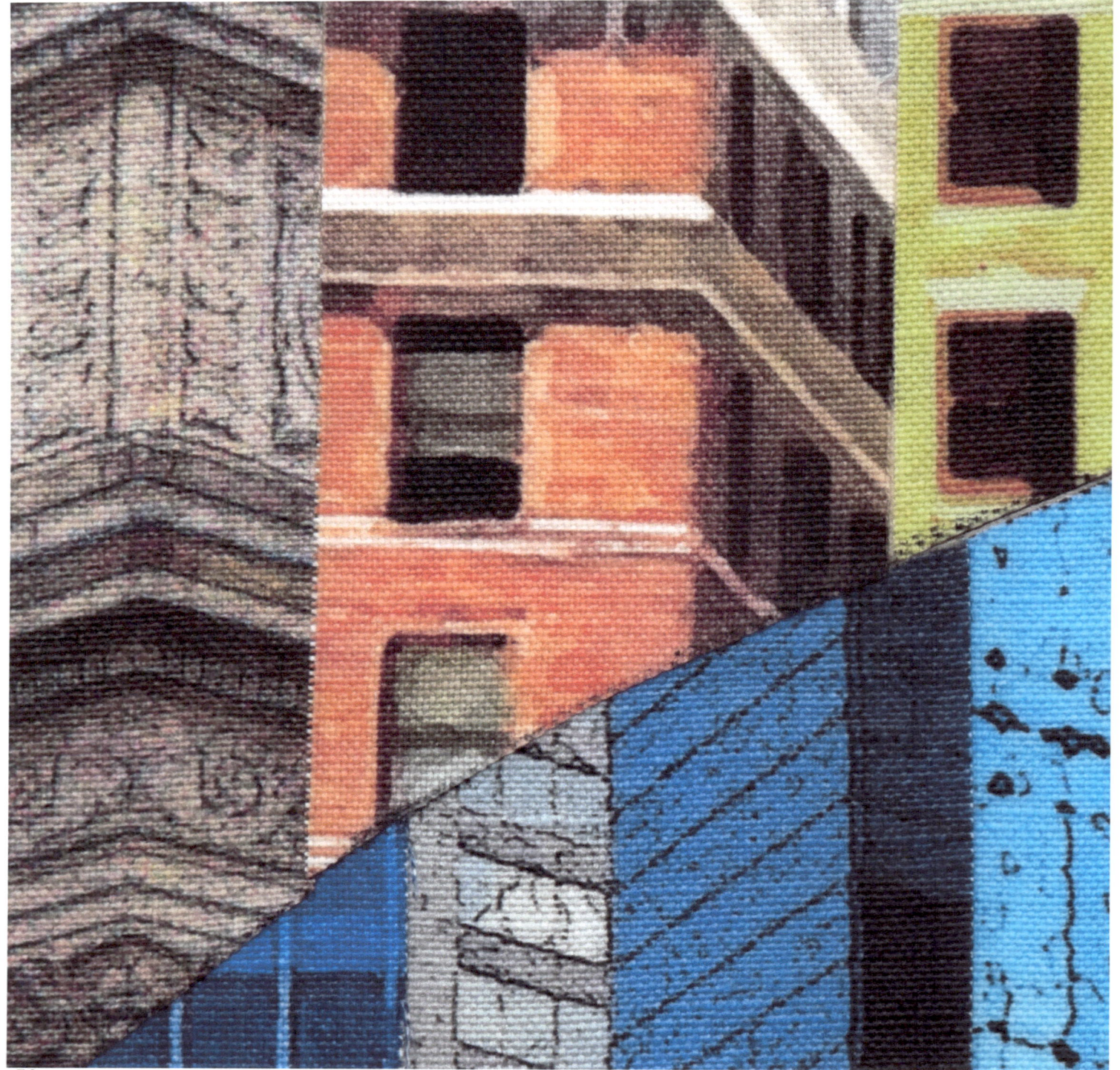

50

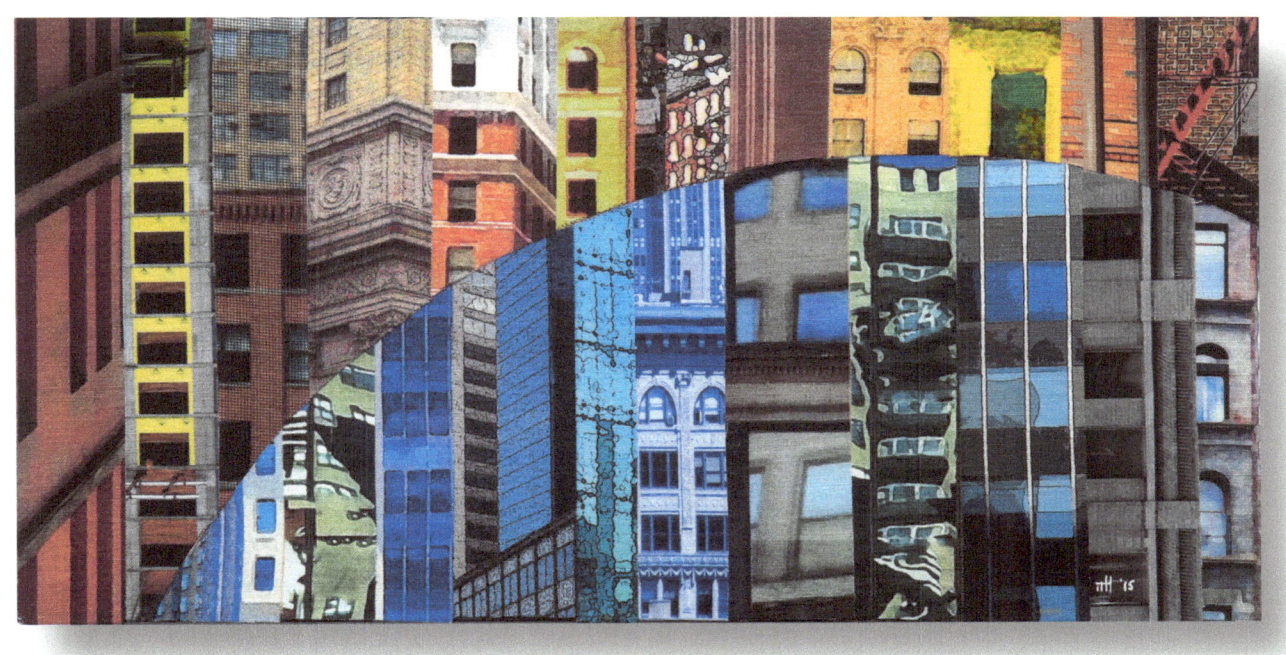

Patchwork City 19.
10"x20". digitally manipulated photography, pigment printing on linen, collage on wood panel

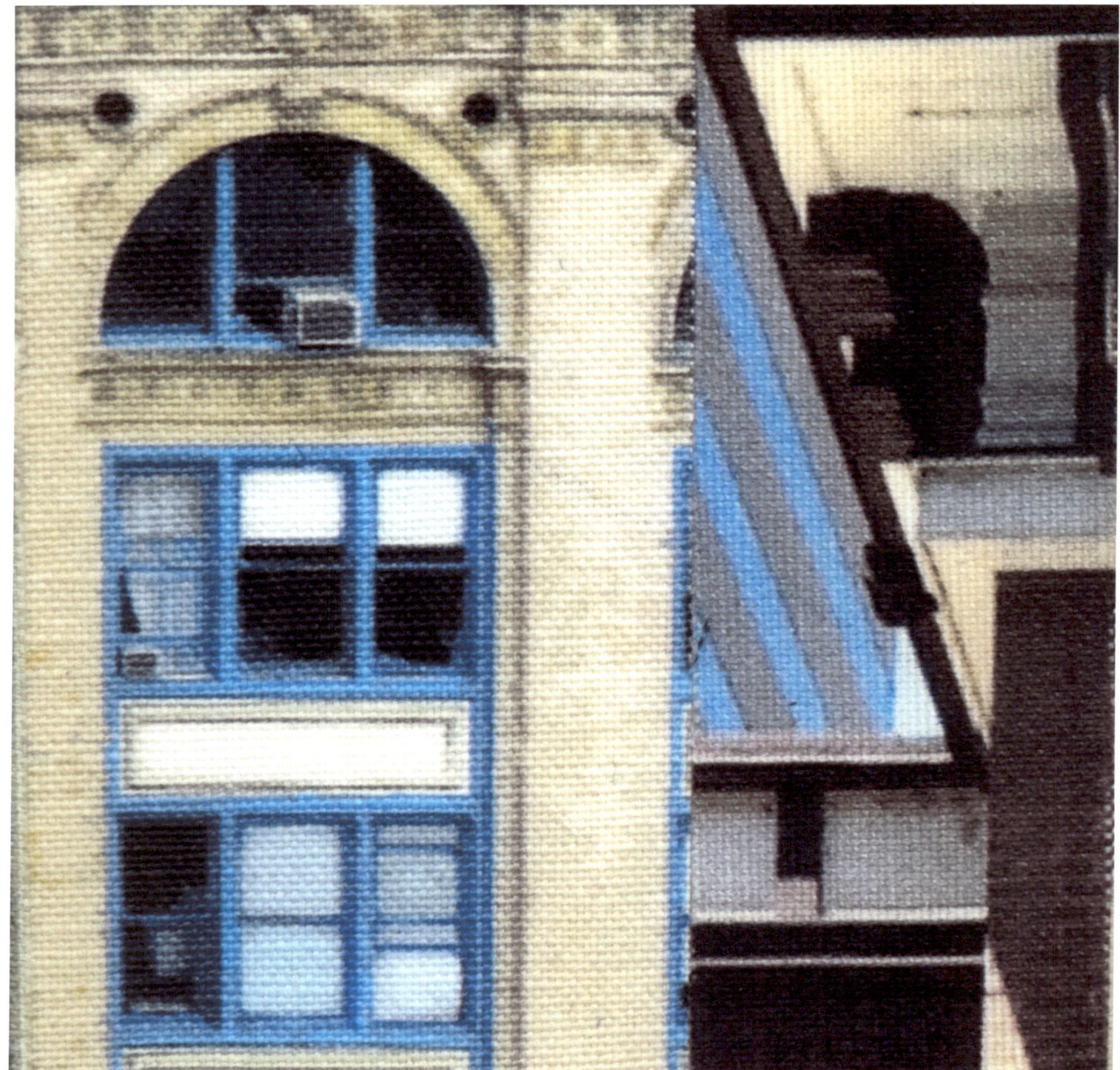

detail

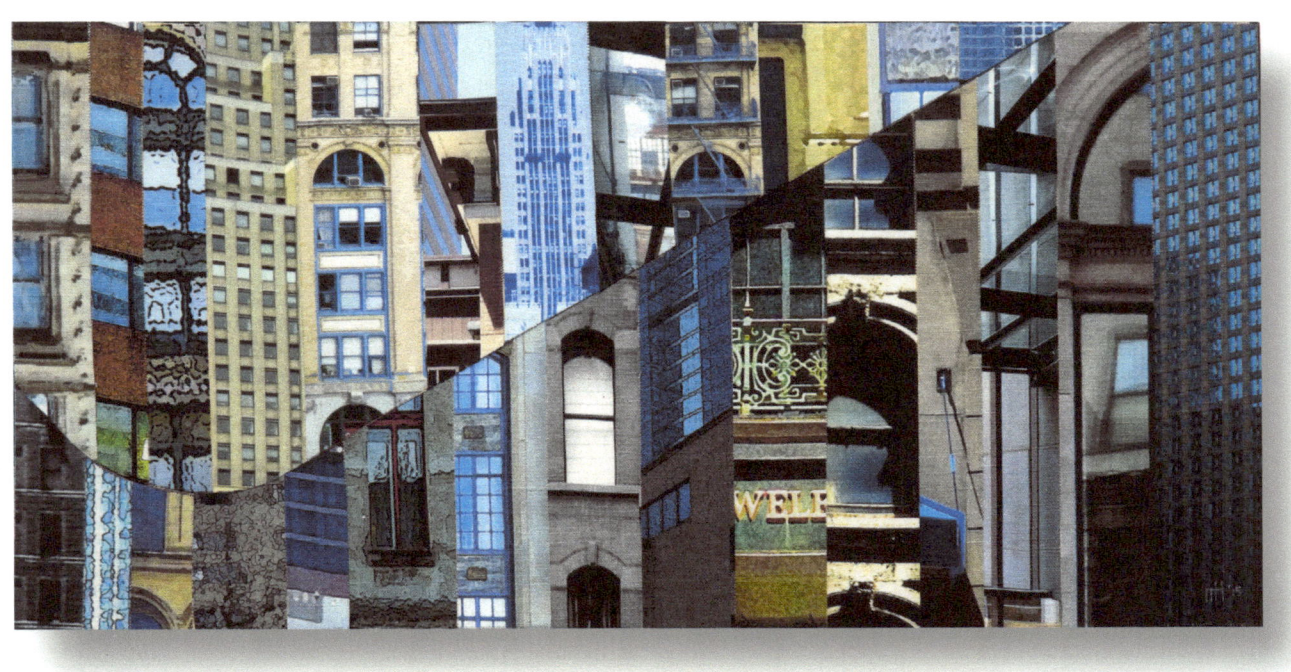

Patchwork City 17.
10"x20". digitally manipulated photography, pigment printing on linen, collage on wood panel

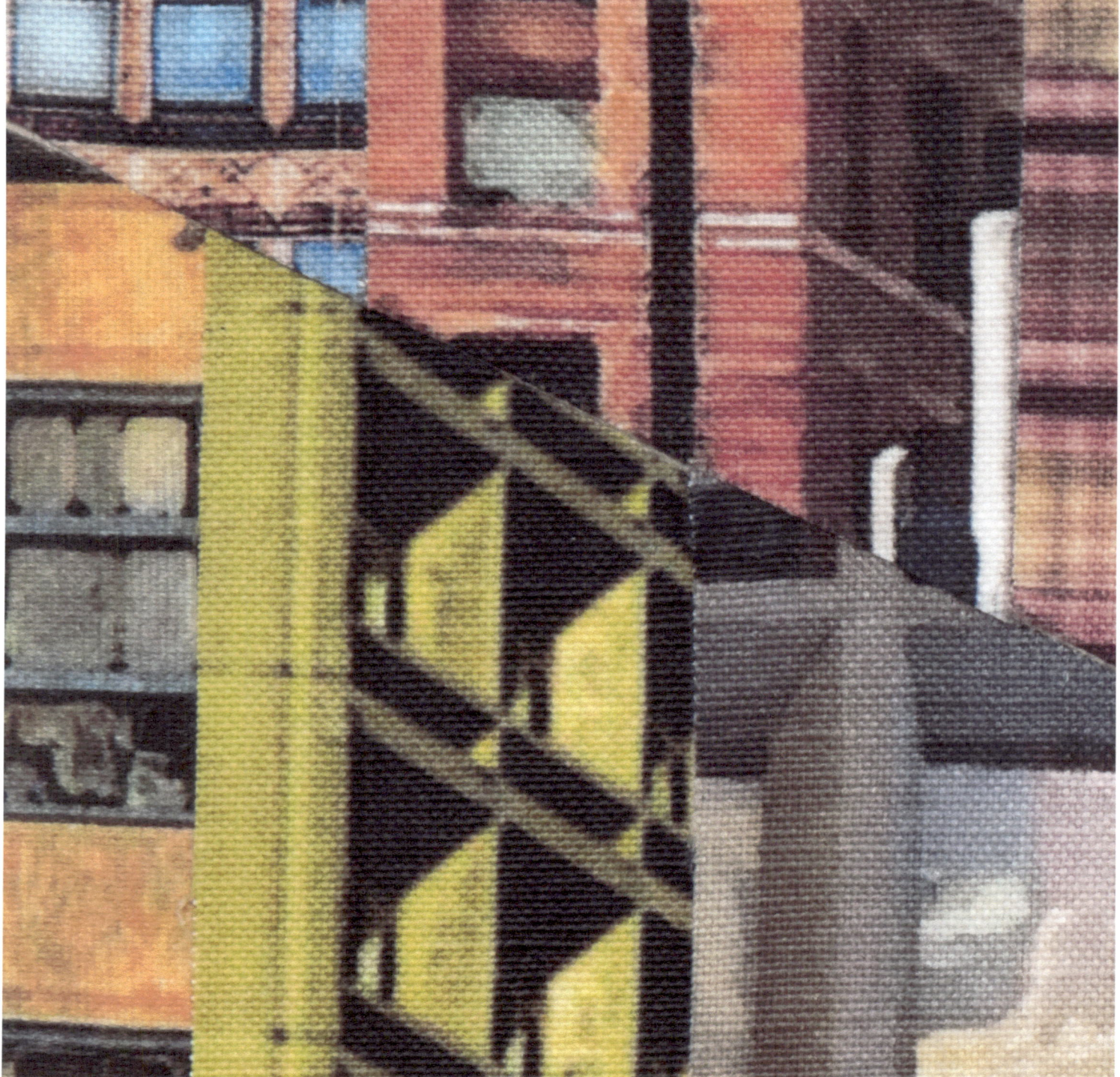

54   detail

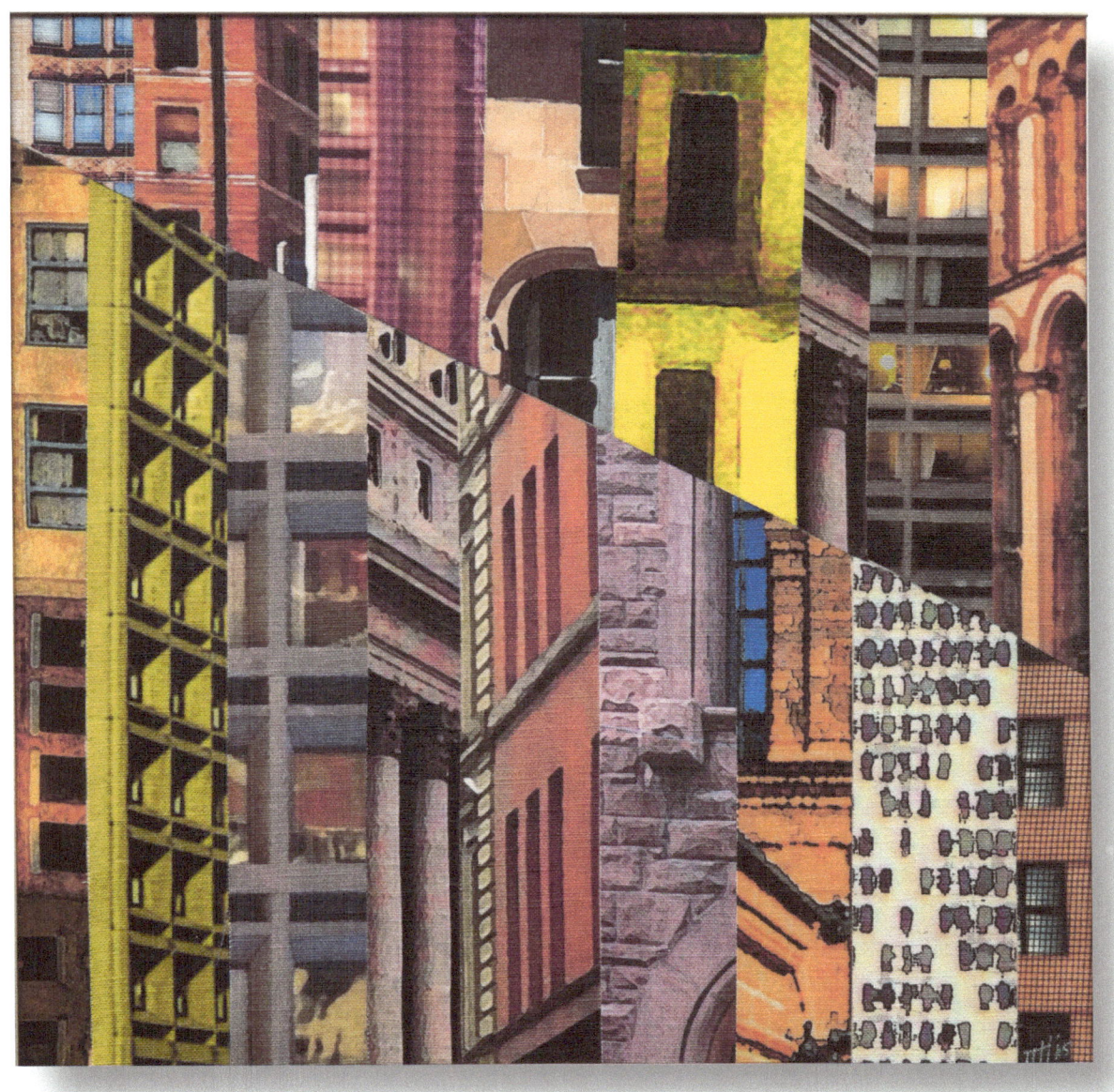

Patchwork City 16.
12"x12"   digitally manipulated photography, pigment printing on linen, collage on wood panel

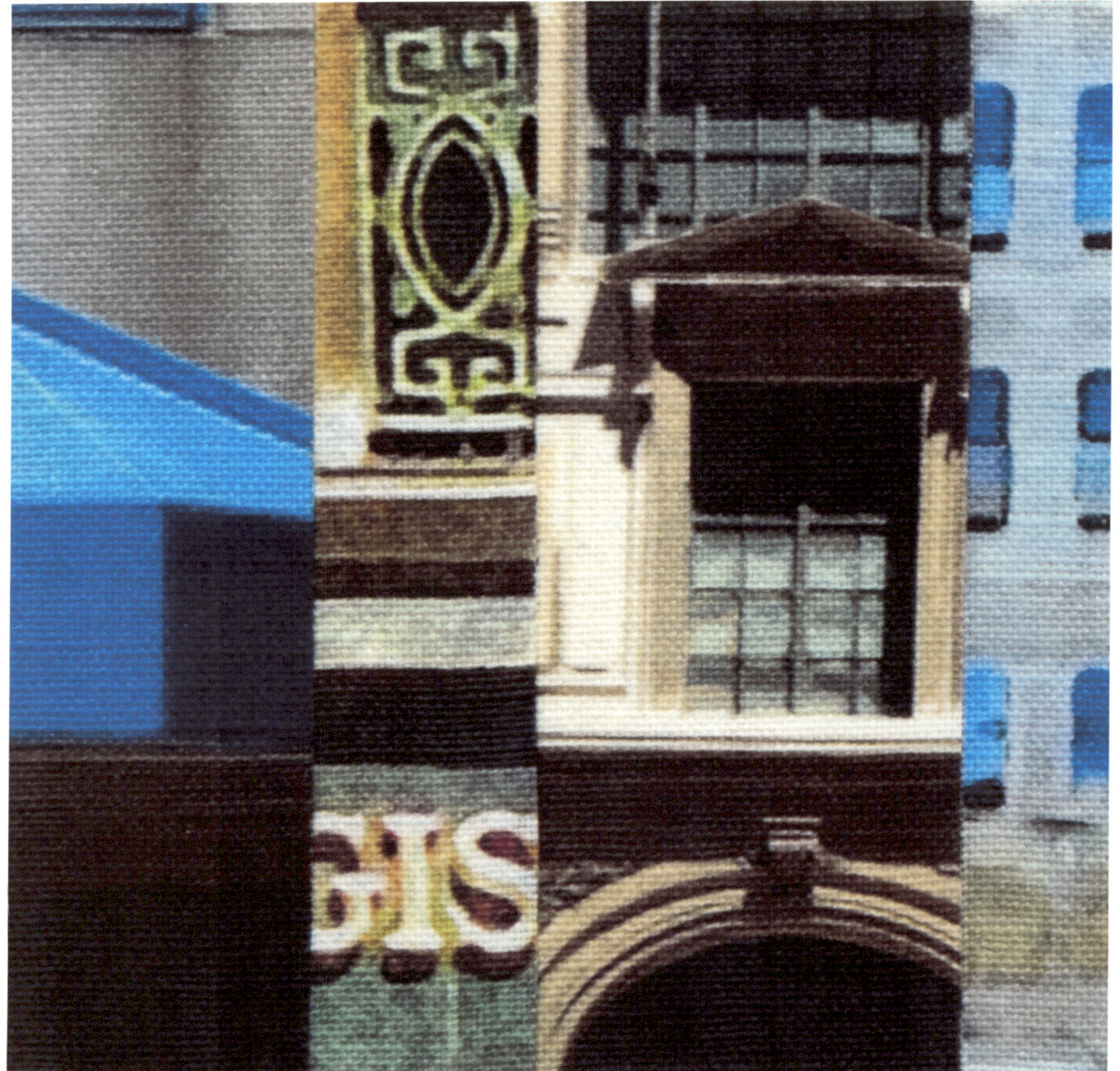

detail

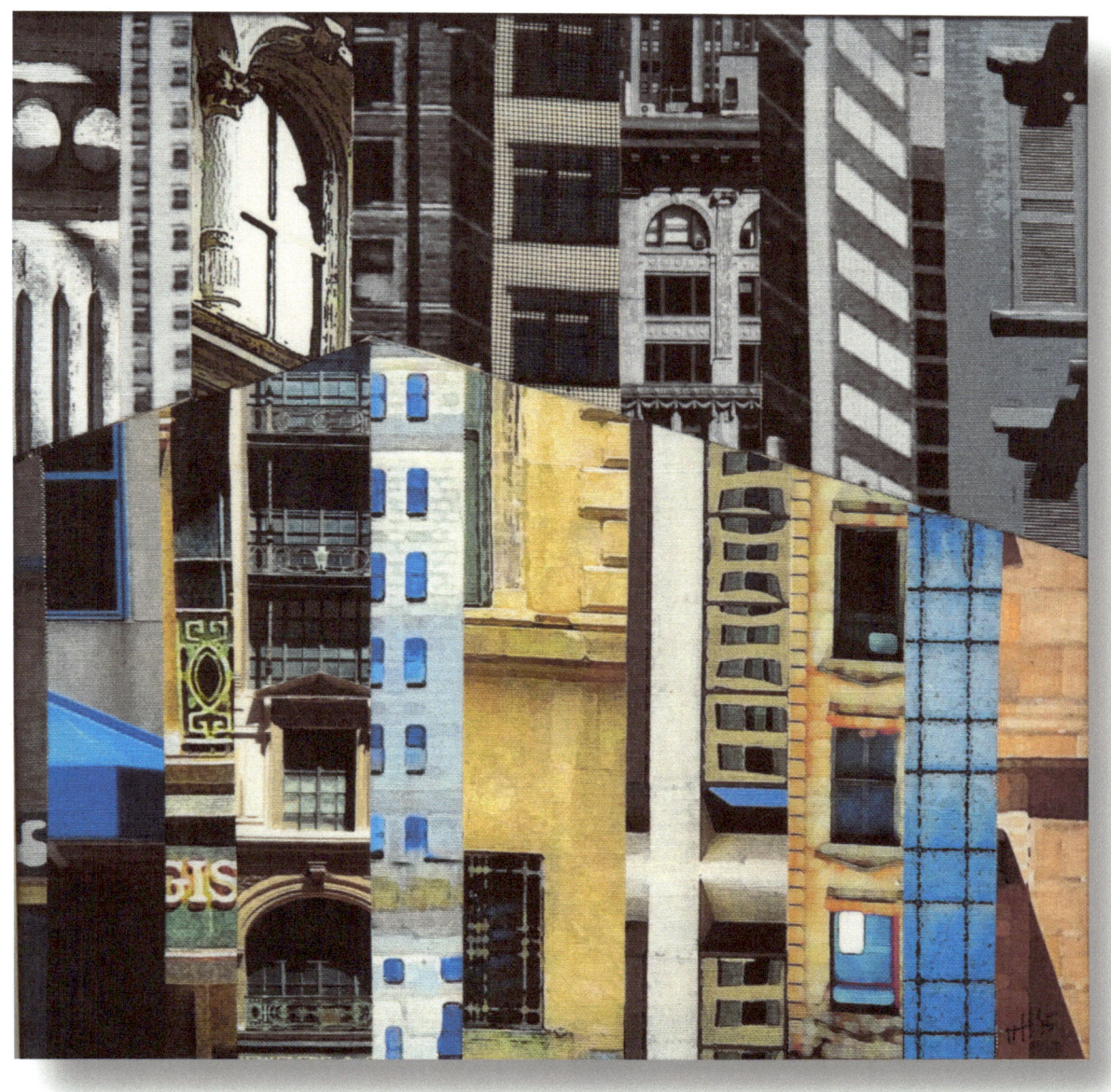

Patchwork City 15.
12"x12". digitally manipulated photography, pigment printing on linen, collage on wood panel

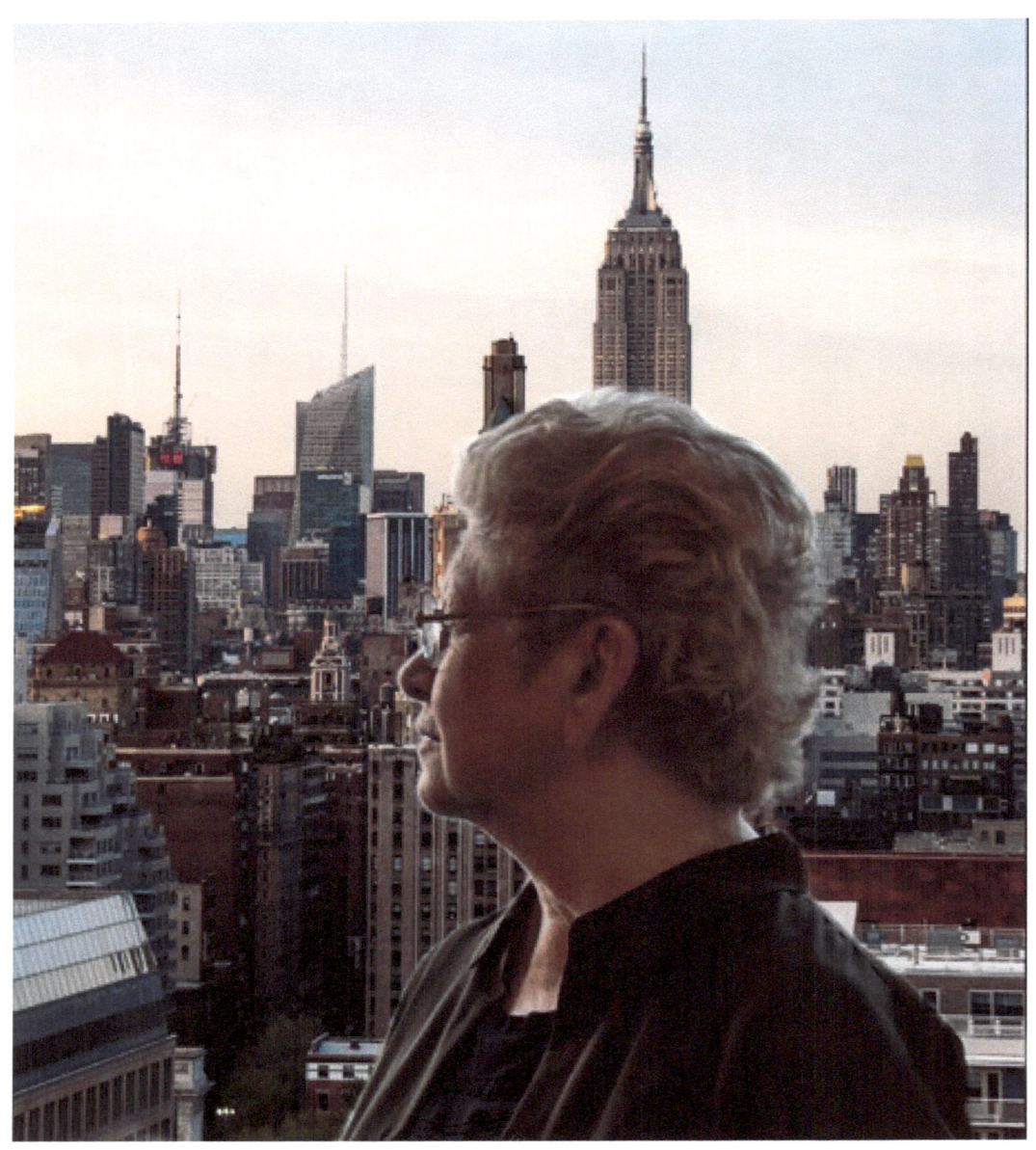

photo: Dan Earle

MARILYN HENRION: CONTINUOUS EXPLORATION

An interview with Jeanne Heifetz for the Textile Study Group of New York , 2017

Jean Heifetz: Have you always been a fiber artist?

Marilyn Henrion: I was originally a painter after graduating from Cooper Union in 1952. However, having four children in rapid succession while working full time kept me from pursuing my own creative work for over twenty years. When I returned, textiles spoke to me in a way that paint never had, and that became my medium of choice.

JH: What was it about textiles that spoke to you?

MH: The tactile quality of the fabrics is greatly satisfying to work with in a way I didn't find in painting. To me, something about the surface texture of the finished work is more accessible and visually appealing than any other medium.

JH How would you describe your earlier textile work?

MH: Up until around 2006, I was creating hand-quilted pieced works. The style was geometric abstraction. My aesthetic was deeply rooted in the urban geometry of my surroundings as a native New Yorker, as it still is today.

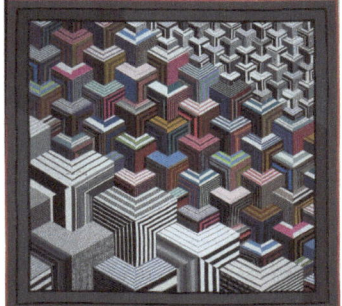

An Immense Journey 1993

JH: While your current work is still rooted in urban geometry, photography now plays a major role. How did that come about?

MH: My creative process is always evolving, and my current work reflects that. I'm still incorporating the method of piecing fabrics that was present in my earlier quilted works, but the more recent works take advantage of new technologies: digital image manipulation and pigment printing on fabrics. Working with my own photographs of urban architecture, I digitally manipulate the images which are then printed on fabric (linen or silk). In some cases, I also incorporate the hand quilting you would find in my earlier works, but I would call the resulting works mixed media rather than quilting.

JH: Are you setting out to photograph specific parts of the city, or are you gathering images more spontaneously?
MH: I use my iPhone to photograph the city as I walk around. Most of the images are derived from the cast-iron buildings of my Soho neighborhood and lower Manhattan, where unexpected visual treats lurk around every corner.

JH: What prompted you to explore this new direction?
MH: I belong to a gallery that gives members a solo exhibition every two years. For me, that means making a new body of work for each solo show. Every two years since 2000 I've explored a new subject or idea, and sometimes a new method of presentation. The collage technique I'm using in "Patchwork City" evolved from the necessity of continuous exploration.

JH: What were you doing before "Patchwork City"?

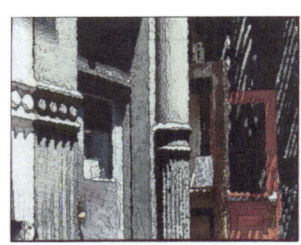

Soft City; Red Door. 2010

MH: In the preceding series, "Soft City" and "Windows," I was using urban images derived from my manipulated photographs, but as "whole cloth" hand-quilted silk and cotton works. I used hand stitching to animate the surface of the works and reveal the city's soft side, the beautiful and complex patina of each façade. The irregular qualities inherent in the materials and construction humanizes the urban geometry. For the new series, I print the images on linen, cut them apart in random strips, and re-assemble them to create collages on stretched canvas that convey the cacophony of ever-changing urban landscape. Although some of the new works also incorporate hand quilting, most are primarily fabric collage on canvas substrate, with no stitching.

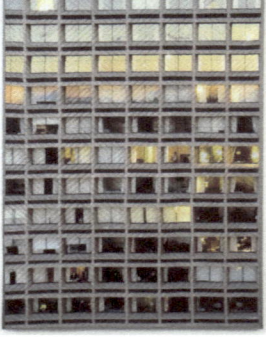

New York Windows.1336 2014

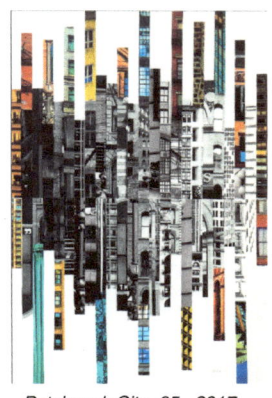

Patchwork City 65. 2017

JH: It sounds like you welcome the challenges of this two-year cycle.

MH: The challenges keep the work interesting: exploring variations on a theme, experimenting with various methods of presentation. And the labor-intensive nature of my methods -- the mathematics of measuring and piecing, scaling a sketch to actual size -- which might be a challenge to some, is a joyful, meditative experience for me.

JH: Do you envision taking the photographic work in any other directions?

MH: I'm finding that my current collage works lend themselves to reproduction very well, especially on brushed aluminum. i am exploring the possibilities of marketing a line of limited edition custom-sized prints targeted to an audience that appreciates my work but cannot afford to purchase originals.

JH: Thank you, Marilyn. You can see more of Marilyn's work on her website. A documentary DVD about her work and life, including her interactions with luminaries such as Joseph Cornell, Claes Oldenburg, Tom Wesselman, and the Beat Poets, is available there.

Jeanne Heifetz, is an artist and independent curator who lives and works in Brooklyn

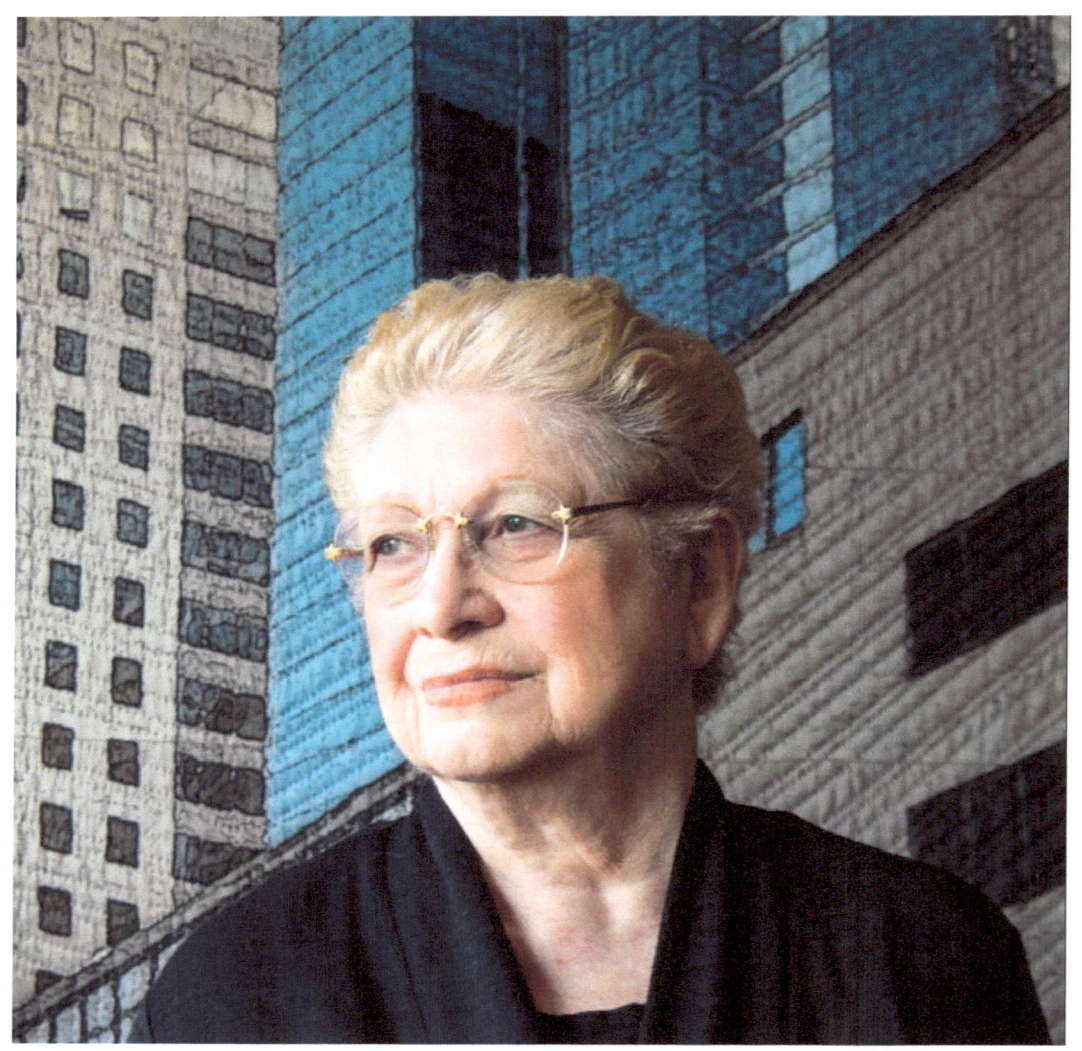

photo: Dan Earle

BIOGRAPHY

Born in 1932, Marilyn Henrion is a life-long New Yorker and a graduate of Cooper Union. She is represented in the Smithsonian Institution's Archives of American Art. After graduating from Cooper Union in 1952, she married fellow-artist and classmate, Edward Henrion, a marriage that lasted 64 years until his passing in 2016, and which produced four children. During the 1950's and '60's, Marilyn and Ed were immersed in the art and literary scene of the era, attending meetings at the 8th Street Club where the abstract expressionists gathered, holding poetry salons at their Greenwich Village apartment where the "Beat" poets of the day would read from their work. Marilyn performed in Claes Oldenburg's "Happenings" and at the newly-founded Judson Poets Theatre on Washington Square. Sunday afternoon visits to friend Joseph Cornell and babysitting by Tom and Clare Wesselmann (then students at Cooper Union) were part of their lives. After retiring from a twenty year career as Associate Professor/Career Counselor at the Fashion Institute of Technology in 1989, Marilyn was able to devote full time to her creative life. Although she started as a painter in 1952, it was textiles that spoke to her in a way that paint never did. Upon resuming her creative work in the 1970's, textiles became her medium of choice. Initially working in the "art quilt" genre, the labor-intensive process of hand quilting added a meditative quality to the aesthetic challenges of "piecing" a work of art that appealed to her. Over the years, Marilyn's work has continually evolved, with a new body of work being created for a solo exhibition every two years since 1999. Her works are included in museum, corporate and private collections internationally. The current mixed media works still incorporate the textiles and piecing that characterized her earlier work. As an octogenarian with unflagging energy, the artist still spends most of her time in the studio, creating new works for her next exhibition as well as for site-specific commissions..

COLLECTIONS

Museum of Arts & Design, New York, NY

Newark Museum, Newark, NJ

Racine Art Museum, Racine, WI

Central Museum of Textiles, Lodz, Poland

International Quilt Museum & Study Center, Lincoln, NE

National Quilt Museum, Paducah, KY

U.S. State Department..U.s. Embassy, Pnom Penh, Cambodia

Mitsubishi Trust & Bank, New York, NY

Nihon Vogue, Tokyo, Japan

Avaya Communications, Denver, CO

Kaiser Permanente, Denver, CO

Lucent Technologies, Denver, CO

Dana Farber Cancer Institute, Boston, MA

Comanche County Medical Center, Lawton, OK

Carnegie Abbey Country Club, Narragansett, RI

SAS Institute, Cary, NC

Rodale Press, Emmaus, PA

Valley Hospital, Ridgewood, NJ

Santa Rita Medical Center, Lima, OH

+ many private collections internationally including Japan, Lebanon, Austria, Russia, USA

SOLO EXHIBITIONS

2017 Noho-M55 Gallery, New York, NY

2015 Noho-M55 Gallery, New York, NY

2013 Noho-M55 Gallery, New York, NY

2013 Durst Lobby Gallery, New York, NY

2012 Noho Gallery. New York, NY

2011 Visions Art Museum, San Diego, CA

     Bayer Corporation, Wayne & Montvale, NJ

     Intermezzo Art Gallery, Bergen Performing Arts Center, Englewood, NJ

2010 Noho Gallery, New York, NY

2009 Bayer Corporation, Wayne & Montvale, NJ

     Berkeley College Art Gallery, New York, NY

2008 Noho Gallery, New York, NY

2006 Noho Gallery, New York, NY

     Galerie Gora, Montreal, Quebec, Canada

2005 Treasure Room Gallery, The Interchurch Center, New York, NY

2004 Noho Gallery, New York, NY

     Studio Decouvrir, Hope, ID

2002 Noho Gallery, New York, NY

2001 Thirteen Moons Gallery, Santa Fe, NM

2000 Noho Gallery, New York, NY

1997 Decouvrir Gallery, Seattle, WA

     La Conner Quilt Museum, La Conner, WA

     Atlantic Community College Art Gallery, Mays Landing, NJ

     Leman Publications Art Gallery, Golden, CO

1996 American Association .for the Advancement of Science, Washington, DC

1994 Merrill Lynch Corporate Headquarters, Plainsboro, NJ

1992 Educational Testing Services Corp., Princeton,NJ

OTHER PUBLICATIONS

WINDOWS, Third Edition*, 2016

WINDOWS, Second Edition, 2014 (out of print)

WINDOWS, First Edition, 2013 (out of print)

Marilyn Henrion: The Evolution of a Fiber Artist (DVD)*, 2013

Complexity*, 2012

Soft City*, 2010

Disturbances*, 2008

Noise*, 2006

Reverberations: Keeping Time*, 2004, reprinted 2014

With Edward Henrion...

Sweet & Lovely*, 2011

Top Hat*, 2011

Book of Chance I*, 2009

*available on amazon.com